AF575104

Just As He Promised

And, lo, I am with you always, even unto
the end of the world.—Matthew 28:20b

Just As He Promised

A Lifetime
Directed and Protected
by the Word of God

Benjamin W. Robertson Sr.

Providence House Publishers
Franklin, Tennessee

Printed in the United States of America

02 01 00 99 98 1 2 3 4 5

Library of Congress Catalog Card Number: 98-65877

ISBN: 1-57736-096-6

Cover design by Gary Bozeman

PROVIDENCE HOUSE PUBLISHERS
238 Seaboard Lane • Franklin, Tennessee 37067
800-321-5692

This book is dedicated to my saintly mother and father,
Anna Mary and Clarence Robertson, whose home
and Christian teachings put me on the right pathway of life;
and to my best friend, my wife, Sugar, who has been
so helpful to me for more than forty years;
and to our only child, Benjamin Jr., who gave
Sugar and me so many happy days to remember.

Contents

Foreword

Robert L. Taylor

THE NEED FOR MINISTERS WHO HAVE HAD LONG-TERM pastoral ministries to put their experiences in print is great and urgent. We have read the works of and have been taught by outstanding writers and teachers who have made positive contributions to our understanding, growth, and development. This is true particularly with reference to those who are aspiring to become pastors of churches or engaged in some phase of Christian ministry. Many of these outstanding writers and teachers have not had the experience of pastoral ministry. Many of us have been blessed by their writings and teachings.

I am very pleased to state that this book, written by Dr. Benjamin W. Robertson Sr., tells the life story of the author and the experiences of a young man twenty-four years of age who was the youngest pastor in the city of Richmond at the time of his call.

This young man who was called to a fine congregation in the city of Richmond, Virginia in 1955 has led this congregation to become one of the largest congregations in the state of Virginia.

When one reads of the life experiences of Dr. Robertson, growing up in a large family in Roanoke, Virginia, working in a restaurant during his school days, facing the problems of the rural and urban churches, these shared experiences should be helpful to young men and women who expect to become leaders in pastoral ministry or some aspect of ministry in the church or community.

Too many of our pastors who made great and outstanding contributions through their preaching, teaching, building churches, expounding and adding to their church structures, have passed on leaving nothing in print with references to their contributions. With their passing and the passing of their contemporaries, much that they contributed will soon pass with them.

I am hoping that many laypeople, and clergy, will read this book which tells the life story of the man who served as the tenth president of Virginia Seminary & College and the founder and president of the Richmond Virginia Seminary while serving as pastor of one of Virginia's largest congregations.

The reading of this book has been helpful to me and I commend its reading to all who may have the opportunity to do likewise. I hope that more of us may leave behind more than "footprints in the sands of time," but printed pages of noble services performed through us "to the glory of God."

Robert L. Taylor, Pastor Emeritus
Fourth Baptist Church
Richmond, Virginia

Foreword

Percy L. High

FOR MORE THAN FORTY YEARS A UNIQUE MAN OF GOD, characterized by Dr. Gardner Taylor, the dean of Black preachers, as one who "wears his worries well," has served the Cedar Street Baptist Church of God as pastor, teacher, administrator, and counselor with dignity and distinction. Under the guidance of the Almighty, this servant has presided over the growth and development of that congregation from a few hundred to thousands of parishioners. He has done this because he believes in what the title of his book does more than imply—that God promised him some blessings which witnesses have seen delivered to him.

The Reverend Doctor Benjamin W. Robertson reveals in this remarkable autobiography, *Just As He Promised*, the benefits of a rich background, proper preparation for pastoral responsibilities, and a spiritual magnetism which have served him well and enabled him to exercise leadership in a church and community in a style that is admired by many in his profession. People are drawn to his messages and ministries because they find in him a man who is able to transform visions into realities as evidenced in sermons of strength and ministries of meaning.

When such a servant as Benjamin Robertson comes along, it is incumbent upon him to share with others the saga of his success. Here we have, in plain language, the story of a pilgrimage based on promises made to one who has led a congregation to erect an edifice as fine and functional as any in this nation and who also founded the Richmond Virginia Seminary where he serves as president. This story should be required reading for all theological students because it is both informative and inspirational.

God may not share with us another like this unique servant of His in the near future. Therefore, let us appreciate this gift from God by reading his story of a journey unparalleled by many because this book reveals to us what God can do with just one person who believes the promises made by God.

Percy L. High, Pastor
Mount Vernon Baptist Church
Durham, North Carolina

Preface

I HAVE BEEN PERSUADED BY MANY PERSONS TO PUT IN words what I feel has been responsible for the almost fifty years of successful ministry. I have held off so long because I wanted the words to be the way that I express myself. Therefore, you will find some long seemingly never-ending sentences. I have picked a few things that I want to relate at this time. However, it must be understood that many times what we want to say is not perceived as we have desired.

I have sought throughout this book to allow the biblical evidence of how I understand God's Word to guide my thoughts. I do feel that my pastorate at Cedar Street Baptist Church of God has been somewhat unique in many ways. I have only mentioned in this book a few of the times that God has intervened when I needed Him most–just as He promised.

I have no bones to pick with the professional theologians and pulpiteers by what I have tried to express; they can fend for themselves. I have written this book for the non-specialist. If one who has lost the sight of his goal can get strength from reading this book and the assurance that God is faithful, then my writing is not in vain. If some man who has not seen that a wife can be very helpful to her husband without becoming a preacher herself, then I have wasted no time in expressing my thoughts. For my "Sugar" has been a wife and friend.

If one is attempting to tell others how to plant and grow tomatoes, then he should take them to his tomato patch. I have not expressed anything in this book that I have not experienced. I invite you to visit Cedar Street Baptist Church of God. While on Cedar Street, you will also see a little struggling seminary, the Richmond Virginia Seminary. You can see for sure that the promissory note is valid, "And lo, I am with you always, even unto the end of the world."

So I send forth what I believe to be true "near eventide," knowing its imperfections, but praying that what's shared here may be helpful to some budding ministry.

Acknowledgments

TAKING THE RISK OF SOUNDING TOO SPIRITUAL, AS A minister of the Word, I would like first to thank the Lord Jesus Christ for making this book possible. If it had not been for the Lord giving opportunity, the door would not have been opened for this work to be published.

I owe a special thanks to some bigger-than-life people: Dolores W. (Sugar) Robertson, my wife of more than forty years; Joyce R. Baker, my sister; Dr. S. Dallas Simmons, president of Virginia Union University; Dr. Robert L. and Dr. Dorothy Taylor, dean of Richmond Pastors and his wife; Dr. Edward D. Jr. and Dr. Clara McCreary, my teacher and his wife; Dr. Percy High, a friend; and Cleomine B. Lewis, editor, *Good News Herald* of Richmond.

My hope is to continue to be a faithful servant of Him who guides us safely step by step through all of life's wonders, challenges and pain. I am honored to have served the pastorate of the Cedar Street Baptist Church of God since 1955 and the presidency of the Richmond Virginia Seminary since 1981.

Just As He Promised

CHAPTER ONE

A Destiny Unfolds

ALL OF MY LIFE, I HAVE HAD AN UNUSUAL INTEREST IN the church. I enjoyed being in Sunday School because I wanted to learn about the people who are considered to be a part of the Kingdom of God. My mother and father, Clarence and Anna Mary Robertson, were dedicated members of the Hill Street Baptist Church in Roanoke, Virginia. We all were very fond of the Reverend and Mrs. David R. Powell, who served that pastorate for thiry-eight years. Our pastor and his wife were in our home for dinner, four and five times a year. My mother seemed to have gotten joy out of cooking at the church and sometimes cooking at home and sending to the church what food she had prepared.

Later my father and mother became members of the High Street Baptist Church during the pastorate of Dr. Frederick G. Sampson. My father served on the Deacon Board and my mother served as president of the Deaconess Board. They continued to serve on the Deacon and Deaconess Boards, respectively, during the succeeding pastorate of Dr. Noel C. Taylor. Dr. Taylor also served as the first Black mayor of the city of Roanoke, Virginia. My parents were married for fifty-four years before my father went to the great beyond. They had lived together so long that mother was never the same after he was gone.

Reverend and Mrs. D. R. Powell.

I had six sisters and seven brothers, and with our parents there were sixteen of us in the family. However, there were never more than ten of us at home at any one time. With that many children, my father had to work very hard. He was a plasterer contractor and that was no easy work. Because of daddy's work, he was not able to attend all the worship services as was my mother. I was with my mother at Wednesday Night Prayer Meetings and on Sunday at the 6:00 A.M. Early Prayer Meeting. The Early Morning Prayer Worship was conducted by the pastor's sister, Mrs. Fannie Hill. So, on any given Sunday, I was in church for the 6:00 A.M. Prayer Meeting, 9:30 A.M. Sunday School, 11:00 A.M. Morning Worship, 3:30 P.M. Afternoon Worship, 6:00 P.M. Baptist Young Peoples Union (which later became the Baptist Training Union), and the 7:30 P.M. Evening Worship. Although I was not yet a Christian, I still enjoyed going to church and being with those whom I thought were the people of God. Since we did not own an automobile, we had to walk everywhere we went. Very few Negroes had cars in the late '30s and early '40s.

However, when I was about seven or eight years of age, we had an incident to happen in Vacation Bible School that disturbed me for months. Right in the midst of Bible study, two of the young teachers began to argue over some materials. Since the church was not able to supply the Vacation Bible School with all of the materials that were needed to carry on a good Vacation Bible School, they had to share just about everything used in the school. It appeared to me, at that time, that one of the workers was supposed to use whatever it was one-half of the allotted time and the other worker the other half. When the second worker thought that the first worker had gone over the allotted time she had to use whatever it was, the second worker went over to take whatever it was before the first worker had finished. When the first worker attempted to keep the second worker from removing whatever it was, a fight broke out. When I saw these two ladies fighting in the church of the living God, I was much disturbed and confused. I had seen fights and had been in fights but never in the church. When I got home to tell my mother, she had already heard it. Bad news travels very fast. I shall never forget how my mother dealt with this serious matter. She let us know that the people in the church were not perfect people and were subject to anger and misunderstanding. However, she did not attempt to justify what they had done. She let us know that the church should not be judged by any of the members of the local church because we are not followers of them but of Jesus Christ, our Lord. What mother said stayed on my mind and in a few months, I had gotten over it.

I thought that when an animal died it was my job to give the eulogy as I had seen the Reverend Powell do. So I would attempt to say some nice things about the dead animal, then I would call on my brother, Jeremiah, to read the Bible and sing. Of course, we did not call it the eulogy, we just said "to preach the funeral." We would fake tears because we thought that one cried at funerals to show their love for the departed relative. Most of the pastors in those days were not seminary graduates. So we had heard that if Jesus cried when Lazarus died that we should cry when our loved ones died.

It was only when I began to study God's Word that I understood why Jesus wept at Lazarus's grave. Jesus did not weep because Lazarus was dead. Why would He cry when He was on His way to awake Lazarus from his sleep?

There are only two occasions in the Bible that mention that Jesus cried. At Lazarus's grave and when He came to the city of Jerusalem. Jesus weeps when we forget who He is. He wept at Lazarus's grave because Mary and Martha did not remember who He was. You will recall that in the eleventh chapter of John, the brother of Mary and Martha, Lazarus, was sick. They lived at Bethany. This was the house in which Jesus was most welcomed. It was Mary who anointed the feet of Jesus with ointment and wiped them dry with her hair. They had seen Jesus do many miracles and loved him very much. So when Jesus received the message that Lazarus was sick which read, "He whom you love is sick," He said, "This sickness is not unto death, but for the glory of God that the Son of God might be glorified thereby." Jesus did not go immediately as you would think that one who loved Mary, Martha, and Lazarus would have done. He remained for two more days in the same place. Then after a couple of days, Jesus said to His disciples, "Let us go into Judea again." His disciples, concerned about Jesus' safety, reminded Him of the Jews who sought to stone Jesus and questioned that He spoke of returning. Jesus told them, "Our friend, Lazarus sleeps, but I am going that I might awake him out of sleep." Then the disciples replied, "Lord, if he sleeps, he shall do well."

Jesus then had to tell them plainly, "Lazarus is dead." And when Jesus reached Bethany, Lazarus had been in the grave for four days. Of significance is what happened when Jesus neared Bethany. Martha came running to Jesus and said, "Lord, if you had been here, my brother would not have died." Jesus responded saying, "Your brother will rise again." Martha said, "I know that he shall rise again in the resurrection at the last day." Jesus then said to her, "I am the resurrection, and the life, he that believes in me, though he were dead, yet shall he live: and whosoever lives and believes in me shall never die. Do you believe this?" Martha said, "Yes, Lord, I believe that you are the Christ, the Son of God, which should come into the world." Martha then called to her sister, Mary, secretly saying, "The Master is come and calls for you." Jesus then went through the same dialogue with Mary as He did with Martha. This is why Jesus cried. Mary and Martha had forgotten that He is the same one who had given the man his strength back who had been sick for thirty-eight years (John 5:5). They had forgotten that He is the same man whose garments had enough medicine in the hem to heal a woman who had been sick for twelve long years (Matt. 9:20).

The other time that Jesus was sad was when He came upon the city of Jerusalem. Listen to Him talking to Jerusalem, "O Jerusalem, Jerusalem, you that kill the prophets, and stone them which are sent unto you, how often would I have gathered your children together, even as a hen gathers her chickens under her wings, and you would not" (Matt. 23:37)!

Chapter Two

The Divine Call

AS INDICATED EARLIER, I WAS IN PRAYER MEETING WITH my mother and Jeremiah every Wednesday night. However, the Wednesday night after the third Sunday in March, 1941, was a great night in my life. I was seated in Prayer Meeting between my mother and Jeremiah when Reverend David R. Powell called for those to come to the altar who felt the need of prayer. Since Jeremiah and I had been so close as brothers, I thought that he and I should go together to the altar for prayer. Jeremiah was a little hesitant when I spoke to Mama to tell Jeremiah to go with me. I shall never forget those words from my mother that night. She said, "Benjamin, this is something that you will have to do by yourself. Jeremiah must make his own decision. Until he sees that he needs salvation, he cannot be saved." Since Jeremiah was almost three years older than I, it was my thought that he had to go first, but my mother's answer was sufficient for me. So I started on down to the front, and as I walked it appeared to me that my feet got a little lighter, as if I were floating on air.

The church went in prayer for this nine-year-old boy who had come forward for prayer. While Reverend Powell was praying, I wanted to get up from that chair and let him know that the Lord had touched me. I had already made my decision while I sat there. As soon as he came to the close of his prayer, I was standing before him as he said, "In the name of Jesus, we pray, Amen."

I knew that something had gotten a hold of me, that something had happened to me that I had never felt before. I felt like running, but all I could do was cry. I was crying and nothing was hurting me. In fact, I had a great feeling of freedom that I had never experienced before. This to me was the turning point in my life. So it was at nine years of age that I gave my life to God. I have never been the same since that Wednesday night almost sixty years ago.

The pastor scheduled the Baptism for the second Sunday morning in April, 1941. There were two of us to be baptized that Sunday morning, the daughter of Deaconess Lucy Dixon and me. The Friday night before Baptism, the Dixon girl notified the officers that she could not be baptized that Sunday. The Deacons felt that since it was Depression time and everything was so expensive, even the water, that the baptizing should be postponed until there were at least two people to be baptized. Of course, I was prepared and had looked forward to being baptized that Sunday. I did not know anything about the controversy until after the baptizing. However, I remembered the talk that Reverend Powell gave to me before and after I was baptized. He said, "Benjamin, usually we have had three and four persons to baptize each time we filled the pool. This time we only have two and we didn't want the two of you waiting any longer. Therefore, we scheduled this baptism for two people. However, one could not be baptized, which left only you. Now it depends on you as to whether we have wasted water or not. If you go forward and live the Christian life and be the cause of others to come to Christ, then the water shall not have been wasted. It depends on you."

When I left church that second Sunday morning in April, 1941, I was determined that no water would be wasted in baptizing me. I was glad that the Pastor spoke up and told those officers—who felt that to fill a pool and use all that water to baptize one candidate when Hill Street was a poor congregation—that it doesn't have to be a waste. It was explained that when there are many people being baptized, it is acknowledged that there would be somebody from the group who would become a dedicated Christian. But when there is only one, everything depends on that one person. I was concerned about what the deacons had thought. The next few weeks, I thought about it often and asked myself the question, "Will there be any wasted water because of me?" I asked God for the strength to serve His Kingdom in order that there would be no waste of water by baptizing me. I surrendered all to Jesus and told Him that I wanted to be more and more like Him in all that I do.

Another interesting thing about my early work in Hill Street Baptist Church in Roanoke, Virginia, where I grew up, was that I wanted to sing. It was not that I had such a fine voice for singing; I just liked singing. Many people referred to me as that little singing boy or that little church boy. I almost lived in the church. There wasn't any worship service that I was not present. We didn't have printed bulletins at that church, but I would listen to the clerk as she would read the activities to be held at the church during the week. I was present to help out with the music. Not knowing how to read music well, I depended on my sister, Anna, who played for me to help me stay in the proper key for my voice. Also there was a schoolmate of mine who would play for me at other times. I can hear myself now trying to sing. As I said before, it was not so much how well I could sing but it was my willingness and availability that made many people call me to appear on their programs. I joined the Roanoke Community Boys Chorus of which Mr. James Chambers was the director and Obbie Saunders was the pianist. Jeremiah and I both sang with this group until it folded. I always thought that the failure of that group was because we had so many things to happen to members of the group due to things that one would not expect Christian boys to be doing. I saw so much un-Christian behavior and so much insincerity that it almost turned me against singing groups. When we would go to sing, the conversation was about how much money we received and how we made the people shout. I am not familiar with the singing groups of today, but I hope that there has been a great change for the better.

Many of my early connections with singing groups were not pleasant. The singing groups appeared not to be serious and went out for what monies they could get. Each concert always had some way to get some extra money for the group. There was always some recent tragedy about which the leader of the singing group would tell the congregation, and after he/she had gained the sympathy of the people present, then the leader would always call for a special offering.

I remember the time that a group made our pastor look like a very selfish, unsympathetic, and heartless preacher in the presence of the congregation. The singing group had written Reverend Powell and told him that they would be passing through Roanoke and would like to appear at Hill Street Baptist Church to render a musical concert. The agreement was to take one offering and to divide it 60/40 with the singing group getting the 60 percent. This was accepted by the group and by the church.

When the day of the concert came, the church was packed with people. In those days, any out-of-town singing group could draw a large crowd. The church did not have a large sanctuary. Three hundred persons could not get in the building. We had a spirit-filled devotional period that was a real spiritual treat. To our surprise, the leader of the singing group stopped singing and began to tell the people about the son of one of the singers who had to have an operation and stated that the singer didn't have enough money for the operation and had no way of getting it. He had the congregation feeling that this was a life or death emergency operation. He called for people who wanted to help to bring him a dollar. A dollar was a lot of money in those times.This is what the singer said, "I am not going to ask you to give what you have come to put in the regular offering that we will take up later. I just want those of you who will give an extra dollar to save this boy's life to do so now. But I urge you to save money for the regular offering."

There were two things wrong with this appeal for the boy's operation. One was that the persons present wouldn't give in both offerings. Negroes did not have much money in those days. Secondly, the agreement was a 60/40 division with the singing group getting the larger amount. Of course, the pastor had to interrupt because he knew that not only would the regular offering be short but the real percentage would be something like a 90/10 division with the singing group getting the larger amount. When Reverend Powell attempted to explain that the church was being shortchanged, there were persons making funny sounds as if he were wrong to hold the singing group to the contract. The congregation thought that he was trying to prevent the people from helping a poor boy who needed an emergency operation.

After the concert was over, the people were so interested in the success of the operation that they contacted some of their relatives who lived in the same city as the members of that singing group. To their surprise, there was no operation involved and no member of this quartet had any boys. It also was discovered that this same sad story had been told at other places and that the the same lucrative response had been received from other congregations.We believe that any servant is worthy of what the people can do for him/her. However, it must be recognized that any performer should receive what is promised to him/her for what has been agreed upon. There is a business side of the spiritual. When one is doing all that his talents permit him for the winning of souls, we must recognize that he/she cannot live on earth and board in heaven. People are obligated to take care of those who serve, especially full-time workers. But the worker owes it to the people whom he/she serves to be honest with them.

It was during my senior year at Lucy Addison High School in Roanoke, Virginia, that what I wanted to do for life became very serious to me. My teachers thought that maybe I was interested in law. For some reason, many people in those days thought that any person who thinks for himself and is able to carry on an intelligent conversation, by all means, should be a lawyer. But what I felt was that divine urge pulling me into the Gospel ministry of our Lord and Savior, Jesus Christ.

Even though my knowledge of the ministry was limited to that conveyed by my pastor, I still felt that there was one and only one thing that I must do and that was to lead persons to Christ. My pastor was not a college nor a seminary graduate, but he was a gifted preacher with an intoning that was as beautiful as any sound that could be uttered from the human mouth.

When I told my mother that the Lord had called me to preach the Gospel and I had accepted that divine call, she told me that she wanted me to be a prepared minister. Therefore, she encouraged me to go to college and seminary because she wanted me to be prepared for the high calling for which I had acknowledged that God had called me.

When I graduated from Lucy Addison High School, I was offered scholarships to matriculate at Morehouse College, Virginia Union University, and Hampton Institute. I also received a full scholarship to Talladega, which included room and board. I had studied the catalog of each of these fine institutions of higher learning and was about to make a choice. These schools represented the very best of the traditional Negro Colleges. With Talladega offering a full four-year scholarship, I was encouraged to make that choice by all who knew anything about the great Negro institutions of higher learning.

I wanted to preach, and to me preaching was something higher and greater than anything that I had ever known. I went to the Virginia Baptist State Convention and heard Dr. E. C. Smith deliver the President's Address, and on the next night, I heard Dr. M. C. Allen give the Educational Address. I listened when these men were presented and one thing that stood out was that both of them were trained at the Virginia Theological Seminary & College in Lynchburg, Virginia, which was just fifty-two miles from Roanoke. I saw these two preachers, in their own ways, electrify that convention. During the convention, we saw a booklet that showed some of the church edifices and their pastors who were graduates of this little school in Lynchburg. I saw Metropolitan Baptist Church with Dr. E. C. Smith, the Vermont Avenue Baptist Church with Dr. C. T. Murray, both in Washington, D.C.; the Pilgrim Baptist Church of Chicago with Dr. J. C. Austin; Fifth Street Baptist Church with Dr. C. C. Scott, Thirty-first Baptist Church with Dr. I. H. Hines, First Union Baptist Church with Dr. J. E. Fountain, all in Richmond, Virginia; Shiloh Baptist Church in Philadelphia with

Dr. W. H. R. Powell; Mt. Vernon Baptist Church in Durham with Dr. E. T. Brown; Dr. Vernon Johns, Dr. W. E. Lee, Dr. James H. Burks and many others.

After hearing these two Gospel giants and reading of these great pulpiteers who were graduates of Virginia Seminary, I gave up all of these scholarships and enrolled in this poverty-strickened school to get an education. In the late 1940s, Virginia Seminary had an enrollment of three hundred students.

LIFE AT VIRGINIA SEMINARY

Since I had never been away from home to live in a dormitory before, I needed someone like a big brother to help me understand college life. My first roommate was Howard Queen, who went to school in the day and worked at the drug store in the afternoon and evening. Since he worked in a drug store that had a lunch counter, he would bring sandwiches and sweets to the room every night. The druggist permitted Howard to take some things to eat to the seminary when he left. Several of us were always around when Howard came to the room. I had never had a problem eating. My daddy used to say, "Benjamin seems never to get enough."

I stayed at Virginia Seminary for two years and received the degree of Bachelor of Theology. Then I transferred to Virginia Union University in Richmond, Virginia. I have not regretted that I made that choice to attend Virginia Seminary. That small school was important in helping me to get a good start in the ministry. Virginia Seminary has dropped a long way since those good old days, and we pray that one day it may regain what it has lost. A school can be no better than the type of students it receives. The survival of all Black schools is threatened if the Black families continue to send their best minds to white schools and the poor learners to Black schools. The Black schools will not be able to train persons any higher than their mental capacity. One of the mistakes that many Black families make is to place a child in an atmosphere in which he has to protect himself from all sides. A student needs friends with whom he can communicate. We had a young man who was a student in one of the fine non-Black colleges who came to our church and stood on the pulpit and cried while asking us to help him finish college. We gave the young man thousands of dollars that morning in order that he may take his test and graduate. His action caused us to have to explain to the givers of our scholarships that all young people were not like that. We understand that he lives in Richmond, and we are looking for the day to come that he will come back to church to let the people who helped him know that he appreciated what they did.

MY FIRST SERMON

So when time came for me to prepare a sermon for the night that the pastor had assigned to me, I recognized quickly that I needed to get closer to the man who had called me to preach. On the campus of Virginia Seminary, there was a walkway between the library and the dining hall in which I walked for hours singing that hymn "Yield Not to Temptation," but it was the chorus that I kept singing over and over, "Ask the Savior to help you, comfort, strengthen and keep you; He is willing to aid you, He will carry you through."

When I came to the realization of what it was all about, the Spirit led me to Isaiah 6:8, "Then I heard the voice of the Lord saying, 'Whom shall I send, and who will go for us?' And I said, 'Here am I; send me.'" I chose for a subject, "Lord, I'll go." When I went to church that night to deliver my first sermon, I told the people about what happened when the king died. I talked about what Isaiah saw, what he felt, and what he heard. The church was packed with almost three hundred people. When I came to the end of the sermon, I just raised my right hand and pointed upward saying, "Lord, I'll go." And I thought I heard a voice coming back saying, "And, lo, I am with you always, even unto the end of the world." Of course, the offering that we took up that night went to the church. The people were asked to give me something when they shook my hand after the sermon.

MY LICENSE TO PREACH

I shall never forget that next Sunday morning when Reverend D. R. Powell called me from the congregation and presented me my license to the Gospel Ministry and gave me a seat on the pulpit. In his presentation, he said, "Benjamin, I feel sorry for you and the young men coming behind you because the work will get harder and harder." He explained it by attempting to show how wicked men and women had become. He quoted to me and the congregation 2 Timothy 4:3–4 (I am using the New Revised Standard Version which was not out in the late 1940s) "For the time is coming when people will not put up with sound doctrine, but having itching ears, they will accumulate for themselves teachers to suit their own desires, and will turn away from listening to the truth, and wander away to myths." When he finished instructing me out of his rich experience in the ministry, I believe that there were very few dry eyes in the sanctuary that Sunday morning. They all seemed to have wished me well. At that time, the church had licensed only one preacher to the Gospel Ministry before me and that was the Reverend Richard E. Jones, who was serving in the pastorate in West Virginia.

After I was licensed, the local churches called on their newly licensed preacher for Youth Days and to sing during revival services. I shall never forget Deacon Oscar W. Jones, who took me to sing at a tent revival service. This was the first time that I had appeared before a group of people who were not Negroes. A few days after I had sung in the tent meeting, I went into one of the dry cleaning shops in downtown Roanoke. I was surprised when the owner of the cleaners recognized me as the young man who sang at a tent meeting the other night. It made me feel as if I had done something great to have been recognized by people who were not of my race. However, that good feeling soon left when she asked me to sing to the people who were in the shop. I was trying to explain to her that I needed a musical background and that the atmosphere was not conducive to sing when the argument started. During the argument, a friend of the family saw what was going on and spoke up and stated that this is not the place nor atmosphere for singing. She took me by the arm and we walked out.

MY MENTORS

I knew that I had to be under a pastor who could help me. So I went to work with Dr. A. L. James, pastor of the First Baptist Church of Roanoke. There were very few pastors in Roanoke in the late 1940s with college and seminary training. Dr. James was one of them. All my life, I wanted to be with those who could help me. Therefore, I sought the company and advice of the experienced ministers, for I knew that a young minister my age and with the same experience as I had could do very little to advise me. Many young ministers make the mistake of going to their peers for advice.

The senior ministers have been over the road in which I was going at that time. Dr. J. C. Diamond, pastor of the First Baptist Church, Berkeley, did much to help me as a pastor of a local church. Dr. Diamond was in his late seventies when I would stay at his home and preach at the church where he served in the pastorate on Sundays. When I drove him around, I would ask him questions and start him talking about his years in the ministry. He was a 1901 graduate of Howard University and had served in the pastorate of the Shiloh Baptist Church (Old Site) Fredericksburg, Virginia, before coming to First Baptist Church, Berkeley. When I was with Dr. Diamond, I was receiving the benefit of fifty years of experience from a successful pastor.

Dr. M. C. Allen, the president of the seminary, and Dr. J. C. Austin, pastor of the Pilgrim Baptist Church in Chicago, took interest in me as a young minister who wanted to grow. I learned about the history of the Virginia Baptist State Convention and the

Dr. M. C. Allen.

Virginia Theological Seminary & College from Dr. Allen. We talked about the future of the seminary and what it would require for it to maintain itself in a society that was changing every day. It was one of the best things that could have happened to me to have been at Virginia Seminary during my formative years in the ministry. I stayed at Virginia Seminary until I received my first degree, the Bachelor of Theology in 1951.

One could not know Dr. E. C. Smith and not be inspired by his wisdom. Dr. Smith was serving as the pastor of the Metropolitan Baptist Church in Washington, D.C., when we became friends. Our friendship lasted over a period of nearly forty years. The depth of our friendship was such that it was I whom he wanted to deliver the eulogy at his funeral. Special thanks to my friend, Dr. H. Beecher Hicks Jr. who was pastor of Metropolitan at the time of Dr. Smith's Home-going Service, for permitting me to deliver the eulogy at the church where Dr. Smith had served for forty-eight years as the pastor. My wife, son, and I traveled with the Metropolitan Baptist Church tours overseas many times. We exchanged pulpits often and were frequent visitors at each other's homes. When Dr. Smith could not go up steps, my wife and I converted one of the rooms downstairs to a guest bedroom and named it "E. C. Smith's Room." When I started the Richmond Virginia Seminary in 1980, Dr. E. C. Smith was one of the first persons who accepted my invitation to serve on the Board of Trustees.

Dr. J. C. Austin Sr., one of the greatest preachers whom I have ever heard, was a great inspiration to me in my preaching. He looked upon me as if I were a son of his. When the Progressive National Baptist Convention meets in a city, the invitation is usually extended to the president of the convention to preach that Sunday morning at the host church, especially when the host church was one of the largest local congregations among the member churches of the convention. In 1963, instead of Dr. J. C. Austin Sr. inviting the president to serve, he invited me to be the guest preacher at Pilgrim Baptist Church of Chicago. He introduced me as one who was standing in his shadows. He also predicted that one day I would be the pastor of Pilgrim Baptist Church in Chicago. I looked forward to the day when I would stand in the pulpit of Pilgrim Baptist Church in Chicago, Illinois, as the pastor. However, when the time came, the invitation was extended from the Pulpit Committee almost as if I said the word, I would be pastor. When I considered, I discovered that Cedar Street Baptist Church in Richmond, Virginia, where I am serving as pastor, was larger than that big church that looked so big thirty years before. They gave me the privilege of recommending a pastor to them. I recommended Dr. Floyd D. Davis, one of the sons of Cedar Street Baptist Church whom I had baptized, licensed, and ordained to the Gospel Ministry and trained in the Richmond Virginia Seminary, to this agreeable Pulpit Committee of Pilgrim Baptist Church. The call was extended to him, he accepted and is presently doing a fine job in that great church and city. Not only have I had the privilege to recommend Dr. Davis to the Pilgrim Church, but I have recommended many preachers who are doing great work in their pastorates. Among those for whom I am happy

Dr. E. C. Smith.

that the churches accepted my recommendations are Dr. E. E. Smith Jr. to the Florida Avenue Baptist Church in Washington, D.C. and Dr. W. Franklin Richardson to the Grace Baptist Church in Mount Vernon, New York.

Another giant who took an interest in me was Dr. Gordon B. Hancock, pastor of Moore Street Baptist Church and a professor at Virginia Union University. I had the privilege to preach at Moore Street one fifth Sunday. When he heard about how well Moore Street had accepted one of his students, he wanted to help me prepare myself thoroughly. I shall never forget his statement, he said, "Robertson, prepare your sermons and the world will know that you are here in Richmond. God has endowed you with an unusual ability to deliver a sermon. You are a steak and not a hamburger preacher. When you fix a hamburger, you have to make gravy for it; but a steak will make it's own gravy." I have tried to prepare sermons which have been a blessing to our congregation. I have never gone to the pulpit without a prepared sermon. After I became pastor of my present pastorate in 1955, I had Dr. Hancock to preach one of my anniversaries on a Sunday morning. The church gave him a check that was more than any of his students had ever given him to preach. He told me when he looked at the check, that he could not at that moment tell me what he wanted me to know; therefore, he wrote me a letter expressing his appreciation for the opportunity to serve and the gift. I did not anticipate that a man who had traveled around the world and studied in England would take the time to write to me. But as I have grown older, I understand. For each time that I have the privilege to stand in any pulpit to preach, I am very thankful to God and the person or persons who gave me the opportunity to serve. For many things that I took for granted when I was younger, now are dear to me.

In September 1951, I was accepted as a junior in the college of Virginia Union University. It sounds childish today, but when I came to Virginia Union University, the feelings between Virginia Seminary and Virginia Union University were not good. I received an inheritance of which I was not aware. I began to feel a little uncomfortable when I mentioned Dr. Allen or Virginia Seminary before certain persons. I received my Bachelor of Arts degree from Virginia Union University and entered the School of Religion at the same university.

In 1951, the Reverend O. D. Brown, pastor of the Second Baptist Church introduced me to one of his members, Dolores Wallace. When I saw her, I knew that there was something about her that I had not felt in the presence of any other female before. She told me later that she felt the same way when she first saw me. However, the time did not come for us to reveal our thoughts of each other until the summer of 1952.

In 1952, I was called to the pastorate of the First Union Baptist Church, South Richmond, Virginia, and remained there for a very brief pastorate. In 1953, I followed Dr. J. A. Brinkley as pastor of the Piney Grove Baptist Church, Virginia Beach, Virginia. For me to have followed Dr. Brinkley surprised many persons because Dr. Brinkley taught in the School of Religion of Virginia Union University. In 1955, "Sugar" (the name of endearment for my wife-to-be) and I got married at Piney Grove Baptist Church, and three months later, we came to Cedar Street Memorial Baptist Church in Richmond, Virginia. We followed

Piney Grove Baptist Church, Virginia Beach, Virginia.

the Reverend John W. Kemp who had served this congregation faithfully for twelve years. During his leadership, which started in 1942, the congregation moved from a basement-type church on Mosby Street to 24th and N Streets. This was a giant step in the history of Cedar Street Baptist Church. However, the congregation was not in the building but two years when God called the Reverend Kemp to the great beyond. When the congregation worshiped on Mosby Street, the name of the church was Cedar Street Baptist Church. When they moved into the 24th Street edifice, "Memorial" was added to Cedar Street Baptist Church and the new name was Cedar Street Memorial Baptist Church. The church has been off of Cedar Street for years. They knew that many would question "Cedar Street Church" not being on Cedar Street. Therefore, the "Memorial" was quite appropriate.

CHAPTER THREE

The Call to Cedar Street Memorial Baptist Church

NO ONE WOULD HAVE THOUGHT THAT THERE WAS ANY possibility of me becoming the pastor of Cedar Street Memorial Baptist Church. There were too many apparent oppositions against me. Cedar Street had made one of their qualifications of the new pastor that he would have both his college and seminary degrees. They would definitely not call a person who had not finished his theological work. Therefore, when my name came in and my resume stated that I was still a student in the School of Religion, the Pulpit Committee would put that recommendation aside.

After the committee had presented a sufficient number of preachers to the congregation, the congregation settled on three of these preachers to be put on the ballot for voting. My name was not listed because they had not given me an opportunity to preach.

A date was set and all was ready for the election of a pastor. The leading candidate just about knew he had the church because the three main leaders had thrown their support behind him and had told him so. Every church has some persons whom the members look to for leadership. These three had that type of respect in Cedar Street. Since everything was now cut and dry, they needed to get some preachers whom they were not really interested in as pastor to temporarily supply the pulpit until a permanent pastor had been elected.

They made a big mistake when they invited that student from Virginia Union University to supply one Sunday. I was happy to get an invitation to preach at Cedar Street because the preachers on the campus had talked so much about this church. So I accepted the invitation to serve. Deacon Willie E. Jones Sr. always contacted the preacher during the week to make sure that he would be at Cedar Street to serve Sunday morning. The church did not want any mix-up and have no preacher to serve. Sugar and I had moved into our apartment, but Cedar Street had my old address. When he called the house where I formerly lived, Mrs. Matilda Holmes told Deacon Jones that she did not know my telephone number but she knew the telephone number of my wife's parents. It was late Saturday night when I got the message to call this Deacon Jones of Cedar Street. When I got him on the telephone, he told me that he was getting ready to call Virginia Union University and ask them to send a preacher for the next day because he had not heard from me since I accepted the invitation to serve, and of course, they did not want to be without a preacher that Sunday morning.

On that Sunday morning in which I had been invited to preach, my wife of a few months and I showed up. Our first impression was not good. The former congregation that sold the church edifice to Cedar Street had not done any painting on the church for years and the sanctuary needed painting very badly. It was a rainy Sunday and the people did not know anything about this Reverend Benjamin W. Robertson from Roanoke, Virginia. Therefore, the attendance was very small in that large sanctuary. I sang "The Old Ship of Zion" and preached, and when I came to the end of the sermon, I closed by saying, "I'll finish it next time." Mrs. Hattie E. Kemp told me later that she was impressed with me the morning that I preached on that rainy day. There were four churches where I had been preaching that were in search of a pastor, namely: First Baptist Church, Berkeley; First Baptist

Church, Suffolk; Zion Baptist Church, Newport News; and Cedar Street Memorial Baptist Church, Richmond.

While I was at Cedar Street that Sunday, I saw the mountains before me, I saw the waters were deep, and I saw the giants, but I also saw the Lord. The Lord had come by that Sunday which made me interested in seeing the other part of the church. So I drove by the church one Thursday night. Cedar Street had choir rehearsal on Wednesday and Prayer Meeting on Thursday nights. I saw an elderly man sitting on the steps of the church. I found out later that it was Deacon William McCree who was also the sexton of the church. Because of his age, Deacon McCree did not recognize me and I was happy because I could talk freely with him about the church. He took me to every room in the church and I began to see a vision for the Lord's work at Cedar Street. My first question was whether or not the church had called a pastor. He told me that the meeting had been set and the candidates had been selected, and he mentioned the name of the preacher whom he thought would get the church. That was a somewhat let down to me because it seemed that everything was already done. Then he spoke up and told me, "Last Sunday, we had a young man to come by that really upset the church." I began to feel good again. Then he continued, "But we will not call him because he is too young and we don't know anything about him."

Miss Mary McPherson (the future Mrs. James E. Harris Jr.) went to the Board of Deacons and told them that the church would make a mistake not to include that young man, Benjamin W. Robertson, on the list of candidates. She told them to call a meeting before the night of the election and add Robertson's name to the ballot. The officers had great respect for her because she was a college graduate. Cedar Street had only three members who were college graduates at that time, Robert H. Kemp (former pastor's son), Mrs. Mildred B. Cheatham, and Miss McPherson. You can see the influence that she had because the Pulpit Committee called a meeting and put my name on the ballot. At that time, I did not know that she was the sweetheart of Deacon

James E. Harris Jr., who really was working very hard for me to be the next pastor of Cedar Street.

Since all the other candidates were highly recommended by Virginia Union University, the committee called Virginia Union and wanted a recommendation for Benjamin W. Robertson. It was a surprise to the committee, when Deacon Harris told them that Virginia Union University would not recommend this student. The school that had so freely recommended the other three candidates had refused to recommend this young man. The committee was further told that if they called that Benjamin Robertson, he would not last two years. I believe that the Lord had to have had much to do with my coming to Cedar Street because it appeared that the odds were really against me.

Second, my bride of a few months felt that we should have remained with Piney Grove Baptist Church for at least a couple of years to show them how much we appreciated the church for having our wedding reception there. Sugar reminded me that Piney Grove had expressed that they wanted to build a parsonage for us and that Piney Grove had just as many members as Cedar Street in 1955.

Third, three of the most influential members had committed to vote for the same candidate already on the ballot. These three influential members had nothing against me because they did not know me when they made their commitment. They felt within themselves that they had to keep their commitment to this preacher because they had known him and his father very well. The committee members were three wonderful people. They had been leaders of Cedar Street Memorial Baptist Church for years. They had good standing in the community, and the people looked to them as persons of sound wisdom. Let me hasten to say that all three became good friends of ours. I have made these series of events a part of this book only to let you know how God works.

When the day of election came, God had already intervened. When God intervenes, nobody can stop Him. After my name had been put on the ballot, the deacons wanted me to have another opportunity for the congregation to hear me because the day that I preached many of the members were absent. None of the preachers whom they had invited to fill the pulpit would agree for me to preach in their stead. Therefore, the only time they had left was to schedule a Sunday night for me to preach. They gave me the Sunday night before the Friday Church Meeting for voting on the new pastor to have an opportunity for the church to hear me preach. After I had finished preaching and sat down that Sunday night, one of the men who had said that he would not vote for me because he was committed to vote for one of the other candidates got up from his seat, came to the front of the church, and told the congregation that he had changed his mind. He said that God had showed him that this boy should be the next pastor of Cedar Street. Those who wanted me began to clap and to say "Amen" with smiles and nods. They knew the influence of this one man. However, this one man would not have been able to influence enough votes because the other two, an influential man and a woman, had not changed, and it appeared that they were not going to change their vote.

That Friday, the voting was scheduled for an 8:00 P.M. Church Meeting with one thing on the agenda and that was to vote on the next pastor of the Cedar Street Memorial Baptist Church. About noon that day, one fine lady, a member of the committee, was rushed to the hospital with a pain in the stomach. The doctor immediately got her stomach in order but told her he had to keep her overnight in the hospital for observation. That meant that since one of the three (I was told) had changed previously, and now this woman who was a strong supporter of the other minister would be in the hospital while the church was voting on a new pastor, it was two down and one to go. Then about 2:00 P.M. that same day, the third committee member, supporter of the other minister, went to the hospital with a pain in the stomach (very similar to the woman's condition); the doctor quickly got his stomach in order but also told him that he had to keep him overnight in the hospital for observation. I needn't tell you that both were released to go home that Saturday morning.

The church met with Dr. W. L. Ransome, pastor of the First Baptist Church, South Richmond. The vote was ninety-four for Benjamin W. Robertson, six for one, and two each for the other two ministers. Dr. Ransome wanted to get the church to make it a unanimous vote. But one of the fine sisters of the church said that she had never seen nor heard this young man preach and she would never vote for somebody whom she knew nothing about. Therefore, the letter that was sent to me stated that I had received an overwhelming majority. In Dr. Ransome's closing remarks, he stated that it seemed as if Cedar Street had already made up her mind and that he was anxious to meet this young man. (We did meet and it was Dr. Ransome's request that this young man be a part in the Last Rites for that Gospel giant when he was funeralized at the First Baptist Church in South Richmond some years later.) I was in a revival out of town on that Friday night. When Sugar and I got back to the apartment, Deacon Merdrith Davis, the chairman of the Board of Deacons, had been by and put a note under the door. All the note said was: "You won," and was signed by Davis. Of course, the next morning, telephone calls started to coming in from persons whom I didn't know by name at that time.

I did remember the persons who were at Prayer Meeting that first time that I went, Deacon William McCree, Deacon James E. Harris, Deacon Merdrith Davis, Deacon Walter Green, Deacon William Jordan, and one woman. The woman was one of the following three: Mrs. Rosa Lawrence, Mrs. Sarah Patterson, or Mrs. Gertrude Christian. Then on Wednesday, I received the official letter from the church signed by Deacon Merdrith Davis, chairman of the Deacons and Deacon James E. Harris Jr., clerk, and was drawn up by the secretary Mrs. Lillian Kemp Mapp, daughter of the former pastor and granddaughter of the first pastor. Mrs. Mapp was a wonderful secretary who worked very faithfully with me and the church until she and her husband moved out of town. The letter stated that the church had voted for me to become their pastor and that the salary would be $60 per week without parsonage. In those days, churches did not sit down and negotiate with a pastor-elect; they made their offer and the pastor-elect accepted their offer if he wanted the church. The church further stated that they wanted me to take over as soon as possible.

Now a problem was created because one of the members of Piney Grove Baptist Church, where I was the pastor, was in a meeting in which Dr. Harvey N. Johnson, pastor, Ebenezer Baptist Church, Portsmouth and I were present. Dr. Johnson, not knowing that any members of Piney Grove were present in the meeting, came to me and congratulated me about the call to Richmond. This is what he said, "Congratulations, Robertson, Cedar Street is one of the coming churches. Kemp did a good thing to lead them out of the bottom. You should do a good job there."

This meant that the news got to Piney Grove that I was leaving before I had the chance to tell them because I lived in Richmond and went to Piney Grove on the weekends.That Sunday morning, my father-in-law went with me to Piney Grove Baptist Church. Sugar didn't feel too well that day, so she stayed in Richmond. When we went by the home of Deacon and Mrs. Edward Hunter (the home where Sugar and I stayed when we were in Virginia Beach), Deacon and Mrs. Hunter said that they were not expecting me to come back. When I asked why they were not expecting me, they informed me then that the people were upset and angry.

They had called a Deacon meeting before the twelve noon worship and had another preacher available to preach if I did not show up. I was surprised that they had called a Deacons Meeting before worship and a church meeting after worship. In the Deacons Meeting, all of the deacons who had worked so faithfully with me felt that there was nothing good that could come about by me remaining the three months. The policy of the Baptist Church is that the pastor would give the church three months notice of his leaving and the church would give the pastor three months notice if they were dismissing him. When people love the pastor and do all they can to keep him, it hurts them worse when he leaves them so soon. Since Cedar Street had called and wanted me to take over as soon as possible, it made it easy for me to agree with them that I could do no more good there. To have to preach that Sunday afternoon was the hardest sermon that I think I have ever tried to deliver. Here is a congregation that usually responded with great emotion while I was preaching. But that day things had changed, I heard only one "Amen" during the whole worship. That "Amen" came when I stated that Piney Grove had been good to me and Sugar.

When the worship was over, we dismissed the visitors and went right into the meeting. I offered my resignation to become effective immediately not knowing that I would not get the three months salary that was due a pastor on his departure. When I discovered that they were not going to give me the usual three months salary, I thought they wanted the wedding money back. So I promised that if they wanted me to give them back the money that they had spent on our wedding, I would send them $50 per month until all was paid. Of course, they were against my sending anything back because that was their gift to Sugar and me. They sat there for minutes with no one wanting to make the motion to accept my resignation. When finally, Mrs. Jakie Hunter, the lady in whose home Sugar and I stayed when we went to Virginia Beach, took the floor and reminded the congregation that they didn't expect me to stay a long time and that Piney Grove could not keep me from going to Richmond. A voice vote was made and I declared it carried. In fact, it was I who presided over the meeting in which I gave my resignation. It was better for all concerned that I gave my resignation at that time. This gave Cedar Street and the Robertsons the opportunity to begin their journey as pastor and people. Here is a pastorate that my school had predicted would not last two years. Those two years have stretched into forty-three years at the time of this writing.

Many people have misunderstood the relationship between Virginia Union University and me. In 1955, a student who questioned a teacher was considered to be unteachable. Those were the days when a student accepted what was taught without questioning. They seemed to have thought it was a waste of time to permit a student to debate what the teacher was saying. As the years came and passed, the relationship was better. I was invited many times to serve in the worship services; such as the weekly Chapel and as one of the preachers for the Week of Prayer during the presidencies of Dr. David T. Shannon and Dr. Allix B. James. In 1997, forty-two years later, Virginia Union University with Dr. Dallas Simmons, president, and Dr. Frank Royal, chairman of the Board of Trustees, conferred upon me the Honorary Degree of Doctor of Humane Letters. Cedar Street Baptist Church of God has always supported the work of Virginia Union University.

CHAPTER FOUR

Early Years at Cedar Street

AT TWENTY-FOUR YEARS OF AGE, I WAS THE YOUNGEST pastor in the city of Richmond. I came to Richmond among many Gospel giants. At the time of this writing only two of the pastors who were in the pastorate of a Richmond Baptist Church in 1955 are still living. They are Dr. Robert L. Taylor, pastor Emeritus, Fourth Baptist Church, and Dr. Edward D. McCreary Jr., pastor Emeritus, Mt. Carmel Baptist Church.

As a bit of history, let us look back to 1955 and see who these Gospel giants were.

The Reverend Y. B. Williams, First African Baptist Church
The Reverend O. D. Brown, Second Baptist Church
Dr. E. E. Smith, Ebenezer Baptist Church
Dr. Robert L. Taylor, Fourth Baptist Church
The Reverend Robert L. Anderson, Fifth Baptist Church
Dr. A. W. Brown, Sixth Mt. Zion Baptist Church
Dr. W. L. Ransome, First Baptist Church, South Richmond
Dr. Gordon B. Hancock, Moore Street Baptist Church
The Reverend H. W. Washington, Sharon Baptist Church
The Reverend S. L. Parham, Mosby Memorial Baptist Church
Dr. J. E. Fountain, First Union Baptist Church
Dr. C. C. Scott, Fifth Street Baptist Church

Dr. I. H. Hines, Thirty-First Baptist Church
Dr. J. J. Woodson, Providence Park Baptist Church
The Reverend Blanche Brown, Bethlehem Baptist Church
The Reverend K. D. Turner, Trinity Baptist Church
The Reverend Isaac James, Fountain Baptist Church
Dr. C. S. McCall, Mt. Tabor Baptist Church
Dr. Freeman R. Berlack, Great Hope Baptist Church
The Reverend J. A. Mosby, St. Paul's Baptist Church
The Reverend Samuel Thompson, Greater Mt. Moriah Baptist Church
The Reverend E. C. Kent, Mt. Olivet Baptist Church
Dr. E. D. McCreary, Mt. Carmel Baptist Church
The Reverend Elijah Turner, Gospel Baptist Church
The Reverend J. E. Arrington, Sixth Street Baptist Church
The Reverend C. B. F. Hinton, Seventh Street Baptist Church
The Reverend A. A. Goodall, Grayland Avenue Baptist Church
The Reverend H. S. Sumpter, Mt. Hermon Baptist Church
Dr. M. T. Fleming, Zion Baptist Church
The Reverend E. H. Bouey, Mount Calvary Baptist Church

As I have said before, the Lord put me in Cedar Street, and I have always believed that the pastor is to be in front leading and not behind pushing. I told God that wherever he permitted me to serve that I would put "preaching" on burner one. I was young and strong, and God had given me a vision for Cedar Street. I was determined to let God lead. In my first sermon as pastor, I told the congregation that three men can ride on a horse but only one can ride in the front. I told them that forty-five persons can ride on a bus but only one can sit in the driver's seat and that if no one bothers the driver or causes him to run off the road, everybody will get to their destination together safely.

So many times, churches ask preachers who are interested in becoming their pastor to write and tell the church leaders what they will do if elected pastor. Really, a preacher does not know what he will do until he finds out what the church is already doing. So when I came to Cedar Street, I began to study the church

Dr. Benjamin W. Robertson Sr., age twenty-four.

family to see what were the positives and the negatives. There were many positive things about Cedar Street.

The first thing that I recognized that kept the church in confusion was the quarterly meetings that they called church meetings. I could not understand why a person who had so much religion on Sundays lost it all when he got in these so-called church meetings. I shall never forget the church meeting we had in 1957. I just sat there and listened and tried to find out why the harsh words, not only to me but also to each other. I remember an elderly lady had been encouraged by those who considered themselves smart to put me in my place. She looked at me and said, "The trouble with this church is that you are hard-headed, you won't listen to anybody."

Left to right—Dr. W. L. Ransome, Dr. Robertson, Dr. M. T. Fleming.

She went on talking, being encouraged by some, to continue to let this new pastor know that they wanted to run things their way. When she finally sat down, I called her by her name and said, "You are old enough to be my grandmother. I am going to respect your age although you have not respected my position." Then I looked at those present in that meeting and said, "We are going to close this meeting and the next time we have a church meeting, you will know how to talk to your pastor." I knew that if they could call a meeting over my protest, they had enough power to dismiss me. If they could not, then they did not have enough persons to vote me out. We went for thirty years before we had another church meeting where all the members were invited to participate.

The Lord helped me to plan a way that His program could be carried on without so much confusion. We organized what is known as the "Administrative Board." Since 1957, the Administrative Board with the pastor as moderator has handled all church matters. The ballot was used for the members of the congregation to vote. Of course, any member could come before the Administrative Board and present what matters for the agenda they desired. We had a deacon to come from another church where the members used the church meetings to say to the pastor and officers anything they wanted to say without any regard as to whom it hurt or how un-Christian it sounded during those so-called church meetings. I told him that Cedar Street met in a church meeting at least fifty-two Sundays a year at 11:00 A.M., and we listened to find out what God had told His preacher to tell us. We believe that the Bible is the Word of God. So we turn to the tenth chapter of Romans which says, "for whosoever shall call upon the name of the Lord shall be saved. How then shall they call on Him in whom they have not believed? And how shall they believe in Him of whom they have not heard, and how shall they hear without a preacher? And how shall they preach, except they be sent?"

There are a few places in the Bible in which the people had a chance to voice their opinion. But if democracy means doing whatever the majority wants, then the Christian church has never been democratic but theocratic. There are some things that are not to be voted on, and they are those that came from God through His called leader. However, a leader owes it to the people whom he serves to get an understanding of where he is trying to lead them. It does not mean that all the persons will agree with the leader but they should understand what the leader is saying. The strength of Cedar Street has been that the Administrative Board has consisted of persons who are well-trained and have been born again. It has been a pleasure for me to have worked with these coworkers whose interests are the same as mine, and that is to do all we can to extend the invitation for others to come to Christ that they can see that Jesus is Lord of all.

THE MAKING OF A FAMILY

We had been at church all day that fourth Sunday in January, 1956. I had taught my class in Sunday School. Sugar and I were in the Divine Worship at 11:30 A.M. and had remained for a Gospel Singing that afternoon. Just as the afternoon singing was over, Sugar said, "Let's go to the hospital." We were expecting, so we called the hospital and she was admitted about 7:00 P.M. In those days, husbands were not permitted to go any farther than the reception area (I am glad that policy changed and husbands are now permitted to be with their wives during delivery). It was one of the saddest moments that we had when I could not be with her at the time a mother needs her husband most. I wanted to challenge that ruling then, but the manager was a member of Cedar Street and I wanted to be nice.

I went back home and waited. I guess I finally fell asleep about 5:00 or 6:00. About 7:30 A.M., the doctor called and said to me, "You are the father of a baby boy who tips the scale at 7 pounds and 14 ounces." I was so sleepy that all I said was, "Thank you." The doctor went back and told Sugar that I was cool and was not excited at all.

After I started to get back in the bed, it dawned upon me what the doctor had said. I put my clothes on and was at the hospital to see what had come to pass. Of all the babies that were there, it appeared to me that my son was the finest. I just kept looking at him and left word at the desk that his name is Benjamin William Robertson Jr. When the doctor came back, Sugar told him that she would get with her husband and let them know what we will

Benjamin Jr., Sugar, Benjamin Sr.

name the boy. The doctor informed her that her husband had already given the child a name.

Benjamin W. Robertson Jr.

I baptized Benjamin at the age of seven. He worked in the church in Sunday School, the Junior Ushers, was a Boy Scout, sang with the youth choir and was very active in the church. Every summer, we traveled extensively. We vacationed overseas each year and have been to just about every state in these United States. To name the countries and historic spots to which we took Benjamin would appear to be bragging. Therefore, I am just saying that he had seen much of the world.

He became a student at Virginia University in Lynchburg, Virginia, and had come home the summer of 1974. On that tenth day of July 1974, Sugar and I experienced something that made us have to lean heavily on our trust and knowledge of our Comforter and Guide. Benjamin and I were preparing for a birthday cookout for Sugar. Benjamin had just left me at the church. He was on his way home with some things for the cookout when a truck pulled out in front of him, and he was not able to stop before he ran into the side of the truck. His death was instant.

The church was not able to hold the friends who came to let us know that they were with us during these hours of bereavement. After the funeral, Sugar and I got ourselves together by being thankful for the eighteen years that we had him with us. He was a joy to have in the home. We surely miss him even now, but we are happy in Jesus and know that one day we shall see him in that Great Beyond. Our hearts were made happy when a group of young people organized a singing group and named it Benjamin W. Robertson Jr. Memorial Choir.

THE MUSIC OF OUR CHURCH

One of the strengths of Cedar Street has always been its music. In 1955, it was not recognized as a strength because many of the members were trying to get the music changed to what they said was real church music. The larger churches of Richmond did not permit any Gospel music in their worship services. The Gospel choruses were criticized severely by many of my peers who were concerned that I would permit such music in the church. One of the problems that I had in the seminary was that I defended Gospel music. Some were trying to say that the persons who sang Gospel music and shouted were illiterate and immoral. They told me that a preacher ought to be able to stand behind the lectern and preach in a normal voice. He needed not to raise his voice because he was talking to people who were not deaf.

One pastor had the nerve to tell me that Cedar Street would not grow. He pointed out the larger churches in Richmond, and it was true that the people in those churches were, for the most part, very quiet while the preacher preached. But I knew that he must not have seen what was happening at Cedar Street because during those early days we had from fifteen to twenty-five joining every Sunday. I knew at that rate, Cedar Street would soon be one of the largest congregations in Virginia.

I did not know how the other preachers felt while they were preaching, but I knew that after I had finished what was on the prepared manuscript that I wanted to celebrate. In the midst of my celebration of what God is and how good God had been to me, there were a whole lot of people present who wanted to celebrate also. The paradoxical thing about the whole matter was that these Negroes were trying to copy the form of worship that the whites had, and the white churches were gradually picking up on the Negroes native emotion. Today, just about all the churches in Richmond have Gospel singing and Gospel preaching and those that have remained stiff have a few elderly persons looking at each other.

You remember the story of the man who was not a church goer. He lived in a little town that didn't have a fire department. The only means of fighting fires was to form a line of persons from the well where the water was to the building that was on fire and another line from the building to the well for refilling the buckets. They would draw water from the well in buckets and would pass the buckets from one person to the next person in line until the full bucket of water was in the hands of the person right at the fire. This person right at the fire would be the person to throw the water on the fire. The empty buckets would be passed back to the well for refills. One day the church caught on fire. The line was formed to and from the building. This man who never came to church before was the person who was the closest to the fire, and he was the person who actually dumped the water on the fire. When the fire was out, the preacher went to this fellow to thank him for what he had done. Then the preacher said to this man, "Thank you so very much for helping us put the fire out. This is the first time that I have ever seen you at the church." And the man responded, "That's true, Reverend, and this is the first time the church has been on fire." I discovered years ago, that if the preacher, along with the officers, musicians, and congregation permit the Holy Spirit to set the church on fire, I declare that people from everywhere will come to see it burn. For more than forty years, Cedar Street has been on fire and people are still coming to feel the heat from the fire.

OUR MUSIC DEPARTMENT

I have always been pleased with the inspirational singing of Cedar Street. When I became the pastor in 1955, Mrs. Ruth Wilson played and directed all the church choirs. She has an unusual beat that was very impressive to me because I had never heard such before. Instead of me trying to get rid of the music that I found at Cedar Street, I felt that the music was one of the strengths of the church. Therefore, I encouraged it and enjoyed it.

Soon after I became the pastor, Mrs. Wilson combined the Senior Choir, the Gospel Chorus and the Roots Memorial Choir and formed the Cedar Street Combined Choir. The Combined Choir under the direction of Mrs. Ruth Wilson has always been a very dependable choir. They lead the singing at funerals and they were often referred to as our standby choir because they were always willing to pick up when needed. How can one forget the voice of Clifford C. Jones, the duets of Mrs. Coretha Seaborn Toast and Mrs. Bertha Ellison, Mrs. Ruth Johnson, Mrs. Eva Hurte, Ted Washington, George Hardy, Mrs. McLena Brown, Mrs. Estelle Jones, Mrs. Rosa Lawrence, Mrs. Josephine Edmundson, Mrs. Alma Dean, Ivory Roots, Mrs. Estelle Stewart, Mrs. Missouri Jackson, and the whistling of Augustine Braxton.

It was in 1956 when the Virginia Choral Ensemble became a singing group of the Cedar Street Memorial Baptist Church. Charles Wood, the president of the Men's Usher Board, invited me to come to his home one evening to hear a singing group that he thought I should hear. When I got to the door that evening, I heard the singing. I thought that probably heaven had a recess and the voices of the angels had come down to serenade me. I just stood there until they finished that musical selection. I sat down and told them how good they sounded. Then to my surprise all but two of the persons who were singing were members of Cedar Street and most of them had been members all of their lives. The piano player was Bill Bennett, who was a member of the Seventh Street Baptist Church, and the other was a member of the First African Baptist Church. I wanted to know their names and why they were not singing at their church regularly. That's when I first met the Virginia Choral Ensemble (VCE). On the first Sundays, we had only the Gospel Chorus singing. Therefore, I invited the ensemble to come and become a part of the singing groups of Cedar Street. They accepted and sang for the first time as a church choir on the first Sunday in February 1956 and have been faithfully serving ever since. (VCE had actually begun in 1947.) On Watch Meeting Night in 1957, Cedar Street was one of the first Baptist churches to have a worship service. The pastor preached and the VCE sang. Also in 1957, we began our first Sunrise Worship on Easter Sunday Morning with the pastor preaching and the VCE singing. The attendance on the first Sundays increased to be the largest of all the Sundays.

The VCE became so popular among the singing groups of Richmond that many outstanding personalities united or worked with them in one way or another. Some of outstanding Richmond musicians who worked with the VCE were Mrs. Marie Goodman Hunter, Dr. Odell Hobbs, Robert Jones, Loretta Smith, Stewart Gardner, and Dr. George L. Jones.

Another outstanding personality in the Music Department was James H. Roots Jr., the only son of the late Reverend and Mrs. James H. Roots Sr. Reverend Roots served the pastorate of Cedar Street from 1917 to 1940 (twenty-three years). James Roots Jr. organized a Junior Choir and the Men's Chorus in 1959 when he returned to Richmond. He had been a part of some nationally known singing groups. The Roots family is a musically talented family. Most of the members of the Roots family could sing and/or play the piano. Mr. Roots could do both.

However, the Cedar Street Male Chorus reached a new height in the coming of Dr. Eric Henderson as the director and organist/pianist. Dr. Henderson is a very talented individual in that he taught in the public school system and could sing and play both organ and piano very effectively. The Male Chorus represents men who are willing to give their talents in the services of the Lord. They sing the fourth Sunday in each month at Cedar Street for the Richmond Virginia Seminary's commencements and convocations. They are very popular in helping churches in revivals.

Mrs. Goldie Gray came to us well-prepared to work in the church from her experience at her former church. She immediately organized the Gray's Gospel Singers. This group is still in existence. However, it has changed its name several times. The Gray's Gospel Singers became the United Gospel Choir, and at the present time, is the Acappella Trio. This group has met with many problems, yet they continue on singing God's praises.

In 1975, the Benjamin W. Robertson Jr. Memorial Choir was organized in memory of our son who met with an automobile accident on July 10, 1974. Herbert Pollard was the first director, and

Herbert worked with the group for a few years until he moved his membership to another church. However, the group reached its height under the direction of Mrs. Gwendolyn Ward and Mrs. Karen Fountain with Jewel Berry as pianist. It has become one of the popular singing groups in the city of Richmond. Through the years, the group has grown more mature in all ways. They sing regularly on the second and third Sundays in each month.

The Voices of Joy began with Mrs. Eva Hurte as the director, Mrs. Ruth Nickens Sayles as organist, and Mrs. Laura Wilkerson as pianist. This group represents the youth of the church from the ages of four to fourteen years. Mrs. Wilkerson served a few years and resigned because of the many activities in which she was so involved. It was Mrs. Wilkerson who had the suggestion for the organization of this group. The Voices of Joy has about eighty or ninety voices representing the largest singing group in this church. They sing regularly during the Morning Worship on the first and fourth Sundays in each month.

On the fourth Sundays in each month, we have the Braxton Singers along with the Male Chorus and Voices of Joy singing. The Braxton Singers consist of members of the family of Augustine Braxton and friends. This family is another one of the musically talented families of Cedar Street.

In 1992, the famous Larry Bland and the Volunteer Choir became a part of our Music Department. This group came to us as one of the best known choirs in our city. They had served for years in one of the large congregations in Richmond. With the already popular VCE and the Volunteer Choir, we formed what we call our Fifth Sunday Jubilee. The two groups render the music on these four or five fifth Sundays in the year. Cedar Street is usually filled to capacity each Sunday, but on the fifth Sundays, we have more people in our overflow than any other Sunday.

I guess the next pastor will have a minister of music. When we receive letters addressed to the minister of music, I have to open the letter and read it to determine which choir director should get the letter. The services of Cedar Street have always been in demand to come to other churches for special worship services, and I did not feel that I should have to wait to find out if the minister of music can go or not. Many times choirs are so trained that if the minister of music is not present, the choir will not sing. I would not know how to take it if I were to accept an invitation to come with our congregation to serve for a special worship service and the minister of music was busy and the choir could not go. When I accept an invitation to come with a choir, I have six choirs on which I may call, and there is always one available to go. Maybe the incident that occurred on a Sunday afternoon with a minister of music and the pastor of the guest church caused me to have the opinion that I have. The pastor had accepted an invitation to come with a choir but because his one minister of music could not come, he had no choir because the minister of music did not want *his* choir attempting to sing without *him*. I have always believed that the pastor was in charge of all the worship services in a local Baptist church. I have believed that the pastor does not gear his sermon to the music but the music centers around the sermon. The sermon is the main feature of the worship. One of the great things about our Music Department is that I get 100 percent cooperation from all of our singing groups. It's not that we cannot afford a minister of music. Paying one person would be less expensive than to pay all the musicians that we have. At this particular time and under this particular administrator, what we have is better for us. If the ministers of music would so train the choirs that they could serve just as effectively when he/she is absent, it may work all right. How would it look if I am not able to preach one Sunday and the church worship were to be canceled because the members couldn't have worship without me?

I remember very vividly when a minister and his choir came to serve at Cedar Street. There was a lady who formerly sang with the VCE but had returned to her home church and was singing with her home church choir that afternoon. She was glad to see me, and I was glad to see that she was singing on the choir at her home church. While we were talking, the minister of music called for all the choir members to come. She was finishing up the conversation with me when he called the second time and said, "I mean come now." She told him as she ran from me that she was talking with me. I was standing close enough to hear what was being said. He told her that he did not care with whom she was talking, when he said to come, he did not want her to say another word but come immediately to him. When I heard that dictator, I knew that he would be fired by me very shortly after he was hired.

TELEVISION MINISTRY

When the news came to us that we could get a spot on Channel 6 television station on Sunday mornings from 7:00 A.M. to 8:00 A.M. for $1,800 per Sunday, we knew that by faith we could do it. Therefore, we began our broadcast and lasted on that TV station for eight years until they decided that they wanted that spot for children's programs, which had been ordered by the parent body CBS.

The members of Cedar Street were initially ready, willing, and able to make the sacrifice in an adventure in which we didn't know if we had any experience or training. We began with Joyce Baker and Kenneth Bishop serving as coproducers with an outstanding group headed by Ronald Williams, Calvin Jones, and Joyce Williams. Many of these individuals continue to serve with the same dedication and energy that started the television ministry. Two of the members, Gail Warden and William Lee, served on the committee while they were not well. They have gone to get their reward, and we have missed them, but they are in the hands of God.

The television broadcast crossed racial, denominational, and economical lines. It has given the community-at-large the value that a spiritual Black church possesses.

Mrs. Baker and Mr. Bishop served well until they were appointed to new positions: Mrs. Baker was made the director of records at the Richmond Virginia Seminary and Mr. Bishop was made the director of the new fellowship hall food service department. Mrs. Joyce Williams is now serving as the producer of the television ministry.

Cedar Street spent almost a half million dollars to get the church to properly produce these broadcasts and spends about one hundred and fifty thousand dollars per year to maintain this ministry. We are grateful to Mrs. Wanda Lewis Goodridge and Deacon Ralph Sterns, who serve as our representatives with the TV station. In September 1997, we moved to Fox Channel 35 at the same hour because CBS had informed Channel 6 that they wanted that hour for programs geared toward the youth.

THE DEACONESS BOARD

In 1956, I organized the Cedar Street Baptist Church's Deaconess Board. I appointed the two first ladies, the former and the present, Mrs. Hattie E. Kemp and Mrs. Dolores W. Robertson, as cochairpersons. We have had four deaconesses to serve in the position as cochairpersons. Mrs. Dolores W. Robertson has served as one of the cochairpersons since the board was organized in 1956. Serving with her have been first, Mrs. Hattie E. Kemp, next Mrs. Bessie Thompson, and then Mrs. Ruth E. Jones. There are two of the original members still serving on the board, Mrs. Dolores W. Robertson and Mrs. Helen C. Epps. Presently the Deaconess Board has a membership of more than eighty members. The members of our Deaconess Board are dedicated in a ceremony on the first Sunday in which they are scheduled to serve. The members of this board serve the Communion bread while the Deacons serve the Communion wine. They are in charge of the candidates for baptism. This is the largest female group in the church. The membership of the Deaconess Board is made up of the wives of the preachers and deacons of the church and selected dedicated women whose husbands may not be deacons.

PERIOD OF TESTING

Every successful leader must pass through a time of testing. My first year at Cedar Street was a period of testing. If I passed the test, I could stay for a long period of time. If I failed the test, I might as well to have sought another place to exercise my pastoral abilities. The difference in ages of the former pastors and me had to be dealt with by the congregation and by me. The late Reverend James H. Roots was fifty-two years of age when the Lord took him home to glory in 1940. In 1942, the Reverend John W. Kemp was fifty-three years of age when he was called to become the pastor of Cedar Street. This meant for the past twenty-five years, the church had had a mature pastor about forty years or older. Then both Reverends Roots and Kemp were members of Cedar Street and knew the members personally. Now I was a twenty-four-year-old pastor who knew nothing about Cedar Street, and Cedar Street knew nothing about me. I did not know how they treated the former pastors who served them, but I soon discovered that they, like most churches, wanted a preacher and not a pastor. I wanted to be preacher *and* pastor. That's when and where the trouble started. But as the Lord built the church membership, it was recognized that this young man had some leadership abilities. Once a people feel that the minister is capable to lead and have confidence in his leadership, the organization will grow.

During one of our regular Deacons Meetings, we had a new deacon (who had come from another church). To my surprise, he voted against my recommendation. This was the first time that this deacon had attended a meeting with our deacons. After my recommendation had been accepted by the board with only one negative vote (and that voice was this new deacon's vote), this deacon made a statement in defense of his negative vote that when he first made it, he did not care for it. He said that many of the deacons who voted for the recommendation did not agree completely with it but went along because I had presented it. He further stated that 85 percent of a pastor's success is likes and dislikes. If the people like the pastor, they will give plenty of room for him to try to make his desires work. If they dislike the pastor, they will block everything that he attempts to do. At first, I almost resented his observation. But after forty-two years at the same pastorate, I am beginning to believe that there is a whole lot of truth in that statement. The success of my pastorate at Cedar Street is because the officers and the congregation have given me plenty of space and time to develop my dreams and visions. A good leader should have the common sense to recognize whether a thing is working or not. If it is working, cultivate it and watch it grow. If it is not working, have a way in which it can receive an honorable discharge. One of the worse predicaments that a leader can get himself into is to get so involved in a battle only to discover that he can't win. He has gotten himself so involved that if he turned around, those whom he had influenced to follow him would think that he is a coward. For him to continue in a no-win situation, he will appear to be a fool.

THE GOSPEL ACCORDING TO OUR ENEMIES

The enemies of Cedar Street have helped it to grow. The rumor got out that "Cedar Street is a big-shot's church and the people who go there think that they are somebody." The only way one can grow is to think something of himself. So individuals who wanted to become somebody decided that this is the church for them. Therefore, it helped to develop a congregation that is not only large but is a well-informed people, a people on the go, a people whose eyes are set on goals. When the congregation outgrew the old edifice, a new sanctuary was built. Our enemies put out that we had built a sanctuary that was too big for the members to enjoy the worship. People who came were surprised that they could sit among fifteen hundred people and feel as if the preacher is preaching right to them and the choirs are singing songs that they would have picked if they were in charge. So they united with this congregation.

FINANCIAL TESTING PERIOD

As I stated before, the first years were testing years of my pastorate at Cedar Street. I had always considered myself to be a good business person. We had an old Packard car that we had gotten the best use out of. It was obvious that Sugar and I needed another car. So we counted the cost of a new car and then made the purchase according to my income. Sugar and I were doing very well in planning. We had moved from our apartment on Rosewood Avenue to the church parsonage, 716 North 24th Street. It was in the fall of 1955 that we decided to trade our old Packard for a new 1956 Custom Royal Dodge with air-conditioning for a cost of $3,600. Air-conditioners in passenger cars were very new. Of course, everybody knew that your car was air-conditioned because of the big tubes in the rear window. Sugar and I had gone over our debts and income very carefully and had reached the conclusion that we could comfortably pay $60 per month car note with a salary of $85 per week. So we traded our old car and got the new car with the understanding that our note would be $60 per month for thirty-five months and the thirty-sixth payment would be a large payment which we would have the opportunity to refinance for another twelve months. Our old car served as a down payment and very shortly, we were riding in our new car. We had the new 1956 Dodge for only three weeks before the bank sent the payment book which stated that we would have to pay $99.14 for thirty-six months. This we knew that we could not handle. Therefore, I went to the car company and told them that a mistake had been made. The salesman told me that the bank refused to give me a balloon payment because of my age. He said that young Negro men twenty-four years of age would destroy a car in three years. I told the salesman that we could not afford the new car at that monthly payment, therefore, I wanted my old car back. The car was still on the used car lot. He said that it could be done but it would cost me $250. I came in with a car paid for and drove their car for three weeks (less than two hundred miles) and now I would have to pay $250 to get my car back. So we decided that we would try to keep the new car. The Reverend Stacy Williams came by to see our new car because he had heard so much about it. He asked us to give him a ride in our new car. I told him that we didn't have any gas in the car. He said, "Let's go get some gas." I told him that I didn't have enough money to put gas in the car. Stacy said,

"Benjamin, you are about the biggest fool that I know. You have a brand new car and can't afford to put gas in it." Sugar and I explained to him what had happened and he understood.

It seemed as if everything were coming apart. Sugar and I decided that we would tell nobody about our problem for we knew that the two of us could handle the situation. The car insurance was higher as we knew it would be, but much higher than we had expected. Therefore, with the car notes and the higher insurance and a baby on the way, we had to do without many things that we wanted. It was a test of our abilities to continue under heavy financial burdens. The parsonage had eight rooms and two baths. Sugar and I moved into three rooms because it made the heating bill less. Yes, we had to pay our own utilities because the church had not grown strong enough to do any better. We purchased 10¢ cans of whiting fish. There were six fish in each can. We would cook three for breakfast and three for supper along with some kind of white potatoes. She cooked two fish and potatoes for me and one fish for herself with potatoes. For lunch, we had bologna sandwiches. Of course, God had not forsaken us because almost every Sunday we ate very well. Mr. and Mrs. Willie Butler Sr. would bring us breakfast most Sunday mornings. It would be our joy when the telephone would ring about 7:00 A.M. on Sunday mornings and Mr. Butler would say, "Don't fix any breakfast, I will bring your breakfast around 8:00 A.M." His wife, although not a member of Cedar Street, would help him fix a variety of foods. Many times we had some left over for the next day. Some of the foods that he would bring would be thick bacon, sausage, eggs, fried apples—they even fixed coffee and sometimes fried fish, or chicken and gravy, or veal, and always hot rolls.

Sugar and I had our love for each other that kept us happy even though we had only the bare necessities. We also had a deep trust in God knowing that troubles don't last always. From January 1956 to June 1956 were months that taught us what it meant to be without. We did not want anybody to know our financial condition. We did not tell her family nor my family. We knew how we got in that condition, and we knew that we would get out in time.

We saw the light of day when June came. Each August, Cedar Street had always given their pastors a vacation check equal to one month's salary. They felt that the pastor would use his regular monthly salary check to take care of his usual obligations. Then he would have a vacation check to enjoy a month's vacation without worrying about his bills. When June came, I told the Finance Committee that I wanted my vacation check now. So I received the first of June a check for $680 ($340 salary and $340 vacation) which we used to pay off all our bills except the car note. Our vacation was at the Lott Carey Baptist Foreign Mission Convention. I believe that I conducted more revivals that summer than I have conducted at any time in my ministry. When the revivals were over, Sugar and I opened a savings account. We had a checking account with some money in it. We hadn't purchased anything but necessities for about six or seven months. We were determined that we would never come to that place again if we could help it. We had money for Sugar's tuition at Virginia Union University. The following year, after Benjamin was born, she returned to VUU to complete her undergraduate work.

The test taught us something that helped us to plan for a rainy day. However, another test came to see if we really meant what we had promised God. During the time of our need, we knew the Bible taught that the best way to have is to give God his tenth of all our earnings. So we began to tithe. This time the test came one Sunday morning in regard to the church's mortgage. Cedar was not paid for and had a quarterly note of $375, which meant that we had to raise $125 per month over and above our current expenses. I did not agree with the method that was used for raising this money, but I was new and common sense let me know that it was better to continue on until the mortgage was liquidated. The note was due on the twenty-eighth day every three months. The church had what was known as a dollar march on the fourth Sunday morning in each month. This dollar march each month usually would be at least $125, which gave a total of $375 each third month. That had worked for about four years with no problem. Deacon Willie Jones Sr. would come to the table and make his appeal and would continue his appeal until the people had given the $125. But one fourth Sunday morning the congregation was very small because of the rain that had continued from Saturday afternoon. It was easy for Sugar and me to be there because we lived next door to the church in the church's parsonage. After Deacon Jones had pleaded and pleaded, we had collected less than $30. We had not raised enough to take care of the quarterly note. Sugar and I had about $200 in the bank at that time. I wrote a check for $100 and gave it to the church. When I got home, Sugar asked, "Did I hear you say that you gave a check for $100?" I said, "Yes." All she said was, "I guess you know what you are doing."

Don't you know that it seemed as if the heavens opened and God gave Sugar and me a blessing. We started receiving from that one blessing, and we haven't gotten all of it yet. Doors started to opening up everywhere. The church started its greatest growth. The dynamic power of the Holy Ghost took over, and in one monthly Baptismal Service, we baptized sixty-three persons. This did not include the number of persons that had united by letter or Christian experience. We had more than a hundred persons to unite in one month. Of course, at Cedar Street, like at all other churches when a large number of persons join, many come in one door and go right out of the other door. It's hard to hold church-hoppers. I knew that many of these persons came because I was the youngest pastor in town. I remember one person (she is old now) who has been a member of about four or five churches, always going where the pastor is the youngest. However, I have noticed that when people have real problems or serious problems, they always seek the advise of the senior pastors. As a pastor who is now over sixty-five years, I get a lot of persons from other churches. During the conference, I do not know that the person has been to their pastor and has not gotten a satisfying answer. Usually they will find some way to tell me before they leave how much they disagreed with the advice received from their pastor and how much I had been able to help them with their problems as an experienced pastor who has seen the morning, noon, afternoon and now the evening of life's day.

I remember very vividly the time that I conducted a revival at a local church during the week. To my surprise, the next Sunday morning, the whole youth choir of that church showed up in a group to worship with us at Cedar Street. Now I knew that the pastor of that church was one of the great preachers of that day. His only problem was that he had been around a long time. There is only one way that one can keep from getting old and that is to die young. Just as sure as noon follows morning, and afternoon follows noon, and evening follows afternoon, the young will get old. There is nothing that one can do about getting old other than to die young. Inside of every boy is an old man who will come out if he lives long enough.

I thank God that Cedar Street still has a very large group of young people. It has an unusually large group of men. We have women, men and children in large numbers. We have tried very hard to make room for our youth, adolescence, young adults, adults, and the seniors to be a part of the whole church ministries. Out of no apparent virtue of mine, God has privileged this congregation to be one of the largest worshiping congregations in this area.

CHAPTER FIVE

Family and Friends

FOR MORE THAN FORTY YEARS NOW, I HAVE BEEN BLESSED with a dedicated wife. She was reared by her mother, Jeanette Holmes, and her stepfather, Arthur H. Holmes Jr. Of course, her grandmother had a great influence upon the shaping of her life. When I met my wife, she was already a dedicated Christian young lady and worked very hard in the Second Baptist Church of Richmond, Virginia. She was baptized by the late Dr. Joseph T. Hill. Dr. Hill was an outstanding preacher and teacher. He was one of the professors at Virginia Union University, and each summer he supplied a congregation in Canada. When Dr. Hill went to the great beyond, the Second Baptist Church called the Reverend Odie D. Brown, who served Second Baptist Church for thirty-six years. Reverend Brown was an excellent preacher who could take humor and develop a sermon. When my wife started to Virginia Union University as a student, she rode with her pastor to the university. He was very fond of her and tried to help her in understanding the Christian ministry. In fact, O. D. introduced my wife to me. I shall ever be grateful to him for that. Reverend Brown passed away a few years ago, and the Second Baptist Church extended a call to another fine young man, Dr. James Harris. Dr. Harris is also a professor at Virginia Union University while he serves faithfully the pastorate of Second Baptist Church.

Dolores W. Robertson (Sugar).

Sugar's congenial personality has made her an outstanding minister's wife, a good mother for Benjamin Jr., and a dedicated teacher at the Whitcomb Elementary School, where she served for thirty-one years. She enjoyed her teaching experience with the five and six year olds. Many times, Sugar and I have met persons who are now grandmothers and they often tell Sugar how much they still remember her as their first-grade teacher.

She was the oldest of four siblings of Arthur and Jeanette Holmes; the others are Arthur H. III, Aleta Grandison, and Lorraine Goodman. The life of the younger Arthur was cut short by an accident. The three females were college graduates. Aleta married Gerald A. Grandison, and to that union came a son and a daughter, Gerald Jr. and Geraleta. Lorraine married Henry Goodman, and they have a son, Adam.

Arthur Jr., my stepfather-in-law, was a nice person and provided well for his family. My mother-in-law was an excellent person to know. She was kind and knew how to make one feel wanted and welcomed in her home. Those dinners that she used to prepare gave her the privilege to express her love for the family. She enjoyed watching us eating her food. She had a way of cooking exactly what a person wanted.

Sugar and her sisters, Lorraine Goodman (left) and Aleta Grandison.

I told you earlier that God gave me my wife. You remember the story that is told concerning the country preacher and his wife who survived on what the congregation gave to them from their farms. The churches in those days did not pay much salary, but the members gave from their farms at least once a year to the preacher's family. There were a man and his wife who would send the preacher and his wife each year some meats. Most of the time, the man and his wife sent the preacher's family some chitterlings, hog heads, pig feet, some neck bones, and a small chuck roast.

One year when the farmer and his wife were about to send some meat to the preacher's home, the man said to his wife, "Why don't we do a little better this year for the preacher? We always send him and his wife some chitterlings, pig feet, neck bones, and a little beef roast." The wife was elated because she had always wanted to send something better than they had been sending to the preacher's family. So the wife went down to the basement and looked in the freezer and got out about two dozen center cut pork chops, about fifteen porterhouse steaks, a few T-bone steaks and a couple of nice round roasts. She put them in a box and folded the top down neatly. Then she called their son to take the meats over to the preacher's house. The father decided to look in the box to see what his wife was sending to the preacher and his wife. When he saw what was in the box, he didn't say a word to the wife, but the boy heard what he said as he gave the boy the box to take to the preacher.

Left to right–Sugar's mother, Mrs. Jeanette Holmes; Sugar; her grandmother, Mrs. Alberta Holloway.

When the boy got to the preacher's house, he handed the preacher the meats from his parents. He said, "Mama and daddy wanted me to bring this to you." The preacher thought it was the same old chitterlings, pig feet, neck bones and maybe a small boney roast, but to the preacher's surprise, he saw those beautiful porter house steaks, T-bone steaks, center pork chops, and a couple of beautiful beef roasts. The preacher looked at the boy and said, "Your parents have sent me all this expensive meat that they could have sold on the markets at a great profit to them." The preacher continued by saying, "You know I don't deserve all this." The little boy looked at the preacher and said, "That's exactly what daddy said. But mama said, 'Let him have it anyway.'"

When I first heard that story, it made me laugh. But when I began to think about it, I thought about my life, a little boy from the hills of Roanoke, Virginia, whom God has blessed with so much. I heard something in the air saying that Benjamin Robertson doesn't deserve all this, but I heard the grace of God saying, "Let him have it anyway." He gave me a wonderful wife, and we had eighteen lovely years with our son, Benjamin Jr. I had never dreamed that there was a church as large as Cedar Street. In fact, Hill Street Baptist Church in Roanoke was my idea of a church. The family which I have, the home in which I live, the wonderful mother and father that I had, the people of all races who gather on Sunday mornings in the main sanctuary of Cedar Street until the ushers have had to bring chairs from the other side, the people in the overflow, the excellent choirs, the ministers who assist in the worship, the deacons who serve so faithfully, the honors that I have received, something keeps telling me that I don't deserve all this but Grace says, "Let him have it anyway."

THE HOME IN WHICH I WAS REARED

My father said that it was on an Easter Monday morning, April 6, 1931, that I came into this world. The family was already a large family when I was born. There were Leonard, Thomas whom we called "Fatmeat," Elizabeth, Clarence Jr., and Jeremiah who was the closest to me of all my brothers and sisters (one had passed at birth). After me came Irene, Anna Mary, Eveline, John, James, Ruth and Joyce. There were fourteen of us. Leonard, the oldest sibling was twenty-seven years older than the baby of the family, Joyce.

Our daddy was a plasterer contractor. He made a good living, and we never went to bed hungry. However, plasterers could not work all the year because of the weather. Daddy made good money from March of each year to the end of November. This means that my parents had to save a lot of what they made in those nine months that daddy was working. My mother was an excellent cook. She could make biscuits that would melt in your mouth. You didn't know whether they were rolls or biscuits. She always cooked enough. We had ten or twelve cherry trees in our yard. During the cherry season, we could can hundreds of jars of fruit. We were able to have some kind of fruit pie for dinner every evening during those winter months.

After school in the winter months, the fun would begin after supper. When the kitchen was cleaned and we had done our

Mr. and Mrs. Clarence Robertson, my parents.

homework for the next day at school, we began our games. Some of us would pick partners for bid whist, some would be playing fiddlesticks, some dominos, some checkers (Spanish and Chinese), and some would be reading. After the supper began to digest, we would fix some bologna sandwiches with sliced tomatoes, lettuce, and a salad dressing. Those were good old days. It seems as if people have forgotten about the family playing and working together. The family was a great inspiration in my life.

When we would go to bed, mama would always say, "Don't forget to pray." My mother was serious about prayer. For many nights, we would wake up and hear our mother calling us by name and asking God to guide us, protect us, and bless us.

My brother Leonard and his wife, Gloria, and their three children lived in Akron, Ohio. He was a plasterer. He and his wife spent a lot of their time and monies enjoying the brothers and sisters of the Masons and Eastern Stars. In his home and in his car, in fact, everywhere Leonard and Gloria went, it was Masons and Eastern Stars. Leonard and Gloria had three children: Leonard Jr., Paula, and Kerita. All three children are college graduates and have good jobs. Leonard is deceased, but Gloria appears to be doing fine.

Thomas "Fatmeat" married Alma Finney. Alma's father was a businessman who owned several places of business on the famous Henry Street in Roanoke, Virginia. When Fatmeat was twenty-two years of age, he lost the sight of one of his eyes on the job at the

Norfolk and Western Railroad Company. Fatmeat and Alma are both deceased. They had no children.

Elizabeth, my oldest sister, is married to Jack Thomas Long Jr., and to that union were born Jack Jr., Brenson, Dana, Reginald, and one girl, Sylvia. Jack is a deacon at the First Baptist Church, Roanoke. Elizabeth was very much like our Aunt Eva, my father's only sister. Our Aunt Eva was a great lady who had a heart to help all whom she could. She has some fine children: Elaine was one of the first Negroes to go the West Virginia State University; Dr. Phillip Rayford and his wife are both educators at the University of Arkansas; Lewis, Hollis, Vivian, and Lorraine were very polished in their behavior, which made it a joy to be in their presence.

My brother Jeremiah and I were very close. Jeremiah was almost three years older than I was. Therefore, I looked to Jeremiah for advice. I remembered when we first got our telephone. Mama would write down her grocery list and would read the list to the grocerman over the telephone. I observed that before she would hang up the line, she always said, "C.O.D." I did not know what C.O.D. meant. Therefore, I asked Jeremiah and I thought that Jeremiah knew everything. Jeremiah said that when mama says C.O.D. at the end of her telephone call that means that she wants him to bring the groceries over today, so when she finished reading the long list, it took less time to say C.O.D. than to say, "Come over today." The next time mama got ready to call for groceries to be delivered to the house, I asked her to let me do it. When I had finished reading the long list, I wanted to show how smart I was, so I said, "Come over today." The grocerman said, "We always deliver the same day that you call in."

When Jeremiah and I were together, we were respected even by the usual bullies. For we fought side by side and it was hard for us to lose. When I started to Virginia Seminary & College, it was Jeremiah and his wife, Violet, who gave me one third of my first semester's cost. Violet is a very kind and understanding sister-in-law. They have two children, Jeremiah Jr. and Andrea R. Thompson. Jeremiah is also deceased.

Irene, the sister just a little younger than I, was married to one of my classmates and friend, Clarence D. Davis. They were the parents of Sharon, Janice, and Linda. Irene passed away some years ago. When she died, it was her request that I would deliver the eulogy at her funeral. I closed the eulogy by quoting the old song, "Good Night, Irene, Good Night."

Anna married Donald Grasty. They met each other when they were students at Virginia State University in Petersburg, Virginia. They are both gainfully employed in the educational system of Detroit, Michigan. They have three children, William Derick, Melody, and Tracy. Sugar and I were very happy when the Grasties asked us to be the godparents of their beautiful daughter, Tracy. All of the Grasties have been very mannerable and kind. All of the children are college graduates just as their parents.

Eveline married Howard Brown, and to that union was born one son, Howard Brown Jr. After the homegoing of Eveline, we lost connections with the Browns. In our attempt to stay in touch, we have made many efforts and all to no avail. Eveline was a nurse and a very good one at her job. She usually worked in the operating room. She was thirty-one years when she met with a fatal accident.

John Henry and his wife, Barbara, have four children, John Jr., Venson, Jason, and Selena. John Henry "Snake" played basketball on the Lucy Addison High School team and in college for the Norfolk State University team. He was slim and trim. When he returned to Roanoke from college, he joined the Roanoke City Police Department. He and his wife decided to make Akron, Ohio, their home, the same city of our oldest brother and his family. In Ohio, he has worked with the Firestone Tire company.

James Bernard (Jimmie), our youngest brother, is married to his childhood sweetheart, Marjorie, and they are the parents of three children, James Jr., Clarence B., and Cheryl. After he and Marjorie graduated from the Lucy Addison High School, they went to Howard University in Washington, D.C. They graduated, Jimmie in engineering and Marjorie in biology. After marriage, they moved to California where they lived until the

My sister Eveline Brown and son.

job transferred to Arizona, and finally to Colorado where he has been for a long time.

Ruth Jeanette attended Virginia State University, and she also went to live in Akron, Ohio, where she met and married Samuel Feaster. They have three children, Samuel Jr., James, and Kimberly. I was happy when Kimberly married and asked me to come to Virginia Beach to perform the ceremony. It is always a pleasure for me to perform marriage cermonies for members of the family.

Joyce was born after most of the older brothers and sisters had left home. Therefore, we did not have the privilege of growing up with her. We saw her when we went home two or three times a year to visit our parents. However, when she graduated from high school in Roanoke, she went to Virginia Union University in Richmond where Sugar and I lived. Of course, she stayed on the campus, and we did not see her often. However, after graduation, she came and lived with us until her apartment was ready. Being a child of older parents, she appeared to have always known how to do things in a mature way. She is married to Howard Baker and they have one son, Michael Jerrod.

My heart has been made happy to have had members of my family working in Cedar Street under my pastorate. I baptized my sister-in-law, Lorraine, when she was a young lady. My mother-in-law served on the Deaconess Board, and my father-in-law was a very faithful member of the church. Joyce, my sister, has served as an usher on the Rosa B. Harris Memorial Usher Board and as one of the directors of the Cedar Street television ministry. She also serves as director of records at the Richmond Virginia Seminary, where I have served as founder–president since 1981. It is good to have relatives living in the same city and working with Sugar and

My brothers and sisters.

me in both the church and the seminary. This has made them very close to us. Sometimes Joyce seems more like a daughter than a sister to me. Sometimes she says that I treat her like I think that I am her father instead of her brother.

My wife comes from a small family in which she has only one aunt, Helena Smith of Portsmouth, Virginia. I came from a larger family with many aunts and uncles. Some of my aunts were Ethel Jeter, Julia, Christine Phillips, Flossie Robertson, Catharine, Eva Rayford. Some of my uncles were Eddie, Jim, Willie Boy, Walter, Buford and Calvin Holland, and Hubert Robertson.

I have referred to myself as an African-European American. My father's grandfather was a non-Black and my mother's grandmother was a non-Black. Then there have been interracial marriages for ten or twelve of our nieces and nephews. We have many members of Cedar Street who are not of African descent (one serving on our Board of Deacons), and we have graduates of the Richmond Virginia Seminary who are not of African descent.

As I write this book, I am convinced that the more we work together, the better we understand each other. At Cedar Street, we do not look at the racial background but rather when we gather to worship, we gather as brothers and sisters and as children of the great God of the universe. We hope the day will soon come to pass "when we will not be judged by the color of our skin but by the content of our character."

Cedar Street Memorial Baptist Church of God.

THE PASTOR'S BEST FRIENDS

The deacons were selected and appointed because the need created the position. To me, the need is still there. I would not want to serve a congregation that did not have some good deacons to help in the ministries of the church.

I like the translation of the contemporary English Version of Acts 6:14.

> A lot of people were now becoming followers of the Lord. But some of the ones who spoke Greek started complaining about the ones who spoke Aramaic. Their complaint was that the Greek-speaking widows were not given their share when the food supplies were handed out each day. The twelve apostles called the whole group of followers together and said, "We should not give up preaching God's message in order to serve at tables. My friends, choose seven men who are respected and wise and filled with God's spirit. We will put them in charge of these things. We can spend our time praying and serving God by preaching."

The Book of Acts begins with how the church struggled with her enemies and how she has triumphed in her victories. But now we come to take an inside view of the administration of the early church. This is what we call "internal affairs" of the church. As the church grew, it began to encounter the problems like any institution that grows. As humans, we cannot escape the friction that sometimes comes during interaction with others. The church on earth has always had some kind of trouble. Sometimes it is persecution from without, and many times disorders arise from within. Don't you know that an inward disorder is always more dangerous than an outward obstacle?

The early church established certain principles and policies which gives her a right to transact business of her own under Christ. The church has always recognized that the ultimate seat of the church's authority came from Jesus Christ and was guided by the Holy Spirit. As the church matured, there was strife among her members. Since the church was constantly having the conversion of new people to come in, and since the church was constantly confronted with the necessity of its maturing, there were problems.

In this early church, there were two kinds of Jews. There were the Jerusalem Jews and the Palestinian Jews. The Palestinian Jews spoke Aramaic. This was their ancestral language and they took pride in themselves that there was no foreign mixture in their lives.

There were also Jews from foreign countries who had come up for Pentecost and made that great discovery that the Messiah had come. Many of these had been away from Palestine for generations. By being away so long, they had forgotten their Hebrew and had begun to speak only Greek. This made the spiritually snobbish Aramaic-speaking Jews to look down on the foreign Jews. Therefore, many of the customs that were observed by the Jews who lived in Palestine were not considered to be important to the Grecians Jews. You see, the Jews outside of the homeland would associate freely with the Gentiles. So you can understand how their brothers at home would have deep feelings of resentment against them because it was suspected that they had compromised their religious principles for financial gains.

The Christian church took over the synagogue's practice of caring for widows and orphans. Therefore, when these two groups of Jews were thrown together in the church, it is evident from what occurred in this chapter that there was a lot of prejudice in that early church. Sometimes I have people who are not of the same racial background as the majority of the members of Cedar Street ask me if they would be welcomed at Cedar Street. I tell them that the Negro/Black church has always had her doors opened to whosoever will come. Here at Cedar Street, we don't look at the color of skin, but persons as brothers and sisters in Christ Jesus.

All pastors need help in carrying out the mission of the church. The preacher has a unique job which can only be carried out by one who has been called of God for that particular task.

In Romans 10:12-15 we find,

> For there is no difference between the Jew and the Greek: for the same Lord over all, is rich unto all that call upon Him. For whosoever shall call upon the Name of the Lord shall be saved. How then shall they call on Him in whom they have not believed? And how shall they believe in Him of whom they have not heard? And How shall they hear without a preacher? And how shall they preach, except they be sent? As it is written, How beautiful are the feet of them that preach the gospel of peace, and bring glad tidings of good things?

A good deacon is a needed helper. Most jobs need a supervisor and some helpers. Usually there are fewer problems if the driver of the car gets in the driver's seat and goes forward. Most of the time if the church is going forward, the pastor and deacons have learned to work well together. The trouble comes when the deacon feels that the church is at a standstill and he attempts to get in the driver's seat. Only one can be in the driver's seat at the same time. I hope that when the time comes that Cedar Street comes to a stand still that I will recognize it and retire. I thank God that Cedar Street has provided a retirement salary for me.

I would like to say something about each deacon, trustee, and deaconess who has been such a great help to my pastorate, but it would take too long to do so. The list would include more than eighty deacons, more than forty trustees and more than one-hundred deaconesses. There is a long list of organizations that have made Cedar Street Baptist Church of God the type of institution that she has become. To list a few: the Nurses Unit; the Cedarites; the Cedarlettes; the Fellowship Ten; LaVie; the Busy Bees; the Floral Club; the Bible Classes and the Saturday Morning Activity Period. We have several ministries: the Minister to the Bereaved (The Reverend Mabel Clark); the Ministers of the Sick (Deacons Calvin Arrington, Harvey Ware, Ralph Sterns, and the Reverend Dabney Bell); the Youth Ministers (Reverends Floyd Davis, Ronald C. Taylor, James Ward, Emmanuel C. Harris, and

Charles Calloway); the Youth Committee (Florence Jackson, chairperson); the Scholarship Foundation (Deaconess Etta Lewis and Mrs. Jeanette Allen); the Scouts (James Ward, Ernest Coleman, Matthew Davis, Juanita Cheatham, Dorothy Nelson, and Louise Vaughan); Baptist Training Union (Mrs. Myrtle Christian); the New Members (Deacon James Cosby, Deaconess Deborah Jones, and Dr. Willie C. Thompson); the Television Ministry; the Radio Ministry; the Fellowship Hall Dining Room Staff; the Prison Ministry (Dr. A. C. Epps, Reverend Emmanuel C. Harris, and Reverend Sanford Williams); and our legal counsel (Attorney Rosemary Harris). These members along with the thousands of other members have made our pastorate a real joy to serve.

During my pastorate, we have had only two deacons to serve as chairmen of the Deacon Board: Deacon Merdrith Davis and Deacon Matthew Witcher. We have had the following deacons to serve as Assistant Chairmen: Deacon William Jordan, Deacon A. C. Epps, Deacon Irvin Burroughs, Deacon Paul Hurdle, Deacon Lloyd A. Jones, and Deacon Leo Scott.

During my pastorate, we have had the following persons to serve as chairman of the Board of Trustees: Raymond Wilson, Deacon A. C. Epps, Clifford C. Jones, Charles A. Wood, Raymond Johnson, Mrs. Barbara B. Kemp, and Charles A. Foster.

Chapter Six

Challenges

IT APPEARS THAT AFTER THIRTY YEARS IN THE SAME pastorate, there arose a group "who knew not Joseph." Many pastors find an eroding of power and respect after that thirtieth pastorate anniversary. We had a young lawyer to join our church family who had been out of the Christian religion for sometime. Richmond was surprised at him returning to the Christian religion by the way of Cedar Street. He attended worship occasionally but was very quiet. Everybody told me to watch him because he had been accused of having a very controversial personality. Cedar Street was getting along nicely.

Cedar Street had had thirty years of successful pastorate under this present pastor. The church had permitted this pastor to be the spiritual and the administrative leader of the church. I was the pastor and also the general chairman of the trustees of the church.

I am not sure as to whether the trustees and some deacons sought the advice of the lawyer or the lawyer volunteered his services. I recognized that some changes had begun to take place in the minds of some of the trustees and deacons as to my authority in the church. To my surprise, one of the trustees said to me when I came up to the Finance Room, "Dr. Robertson, according to our lawyer, you have no business in this room. Your job is to look after the spiritual affairs of the church. This is the job of the trustees." My response was that I was both pastor and a trustee, which qualified me under any rule. This was the first time that I had heard that a lawyer was involved. I heard what he said but felt it was too early for me to respond to him. I needed more information as to where and how this legal advice came about.

The next thing that happened was that this lawyer prepared a court order to have my name taken off of the list of trustees. The document was prepared by a lawyer; therefore, it was correctly done. There was a meeting of the trustees, and the person whom I had accepted to serve as chairman served as moderator, and the secretary of the Trustee Board served as church clerk. However, when it came before the judge to order the change in the list of trustees for Cedar Street Memorial Baptist Church, there was a concern as to why a document is prepared that first, removed the name of Dr. Benjamin W. Robertson (which was listed on the court records); second, the document was not signed by him as pastor nor the clerk of the church; and third, the document had the name of a trustee serving as moderator and a trustee serving as the church clerk. Therefore, the judge wanted to know why the names of the pastor and clerk were left off. The lawyer attempted to inform the judge that the Trustee Board of Cedar Street was a self-perpetuating board. But the judge was too smart to buy that. In the judge's rejection of this brilliant lawyer's attempt to have the pastor's name deleted from the trustees of Cedar Street, the pastor was notified of this attempt. It angered many of the good members of Cedar Street that there was a possibility that the pastor's name could have been removed from the court-appointed trustees and the pastor and the church would not have known about it. The pastor had been made a trustee because the church needed a person with some financial backing to lead in securing the loan from the bank. The loan was nearly paid off, and now these persons who sought him when they needed his financial strength felt that he was no longer needed on the board of trustees.

I knew then that this group would continue because they had organized. They had persuaded some good deacons and members that the power of the pulpit should be reduced. I had led this congregation to be one of the strongest in the state. For some reason they had gathered many with doctorate and master's degrees in their fields to do all they could to put this preacher in what they thought was his rightful place. God told me to let them see that they could not direct the program of Cedar Street from their workplaces as well as I could on the scene.

Deacon Robert Kemp, (son of the former pastor and grandson of the first pastor) the chairman of the Finance Committee, Clifford Jones, chairman of the trustees, and I had worked together very well. Deacon Kemp, trustee Jones, and I decided that we should let them direct the finances and the administrative work of the church with the help of their lawyer. Deacon Robert Kemp resigned from the Finance Committee, Trustee Clifford Jones resigned from the Board of Trustees, and I appointed one with a doctorate degree who had been most critical of us as the chairmen. I knew with all of his training, he did not know how to be the pastor of Cedar Street. At the same meeting, we turned over the control of the finances to this committee who thought that they could do a better job than we were doing. At the time, we turned over a bank book; the church had almost $60,000. With a smile, I told them they had enough money to do a good job. We informed the church family on Sunday morning who the new leaders were. The church did not like it because they had seen many years of progress with these three persons (Robertson, Kemp, Jones) directing the financial work of the church. This was done on the first Sunday in September 1986. As any church leader knows, the vacation months (June, July, and August) are usually the months in which the church's offerings are the smallest. Therefore, September was the beginning of the largest offerings until June of the next year. With the church Anniversary Offering of $35,000, they had $95,000 and should have done a good job.

I don't believe that there was any dishonesty, but God had not given them the wisdom and the vision to direct the program of the church. God gave that to me. When I discovered in February that the Church Treasury was down to less than $15,000, I knew then that I had to come back and conduct the finances of the church. So I called a meeting with the church to let the Cedar Street Church family state by vote of the congregation the person or persons whom they wanted to be in charge of directing the finances of the church. The thing that was disturbing to me and others was that these persons had persuaded a few nice people to think that they could do better because so many of them were very highly trained in their respective fields.

Since we had not had an old fashioned church meeting in almost thirty years, the congregation knew that it must have been something very serious for me to call a meeting. On March 21, 1987, at 1:00 P.M., I called the church for a conference for one purpose, and that was to put on record the person or persons whom the church members wanted to be their leader.

To my surprise, there was an opened letter that was being passed throughout the congregation attempting to make this group look good and for Robertson, Kemp, and Jones to look bad. This letter was composed by one man who soon discovered that he had taken a tiger by the tail and not a little kitten. Most of the people who had given him an ear were very disappointed in him for attempting to take the credit from a leader who had led a small congregation into one of the largest in the state. A leader's strength is shown in the success of his work. The members of Cedar Street showed these wanting-to-be leaders how they felt about them and their lawyer by giving the pastor authorities far beyond what the average Baptist church gives their pastor. They discovered that my training, my experience, and my calling of God to be the leader of Cedar Street Baptist family made this educator and his committee almost helpless in trying to persuade the members who attended the church conference to let them stay in charge.

Whenever there are conditions that would destroy the unity of the church if left to work itself out, someone must be given the authority to solve it. World War II would not have ended so quickly if we had not had the atomic bomb. The A-bomb produced an explosion equal to that of twenty thousand tons of TNT. Within a week after testing, the American planes helped bring World War II to an end by dropping atomic bombs on Hiroshima and Nagasaki, Japan. The fact that a single plane could deliver such a destructive device was what was needed to bring the enemies down quickly. Cedar Street gave me such authority that it was not possible for any single group to stand up against such authority. Without this immediate power, Cedar Street could have been in for years of inward fighting. They had the option to have given me temporary power, but they gave this power for the duration of my pastorate. God forbid that this would be abused. Take a look at the minutes of this church conference.

MINUTES OF THE CHURCH CONFERENCE
MARCH 21, 1987

The Cedar Street Church Family met on Saturday, March 21, 1987, at 1:00 P.M. in the Main Sanctuary of the church to put on record the person or persons whom the church wanted to be in charge of her activities. Prayer was offered by Dr. Phillip Williams. There were 368 persons present. The meeting was called to order by the Moderator, Dr. Benjamin W. Robertson.

The reason for this meeting is that there were a few persons who had questioned the pastor's authority because the records of the church were not clear on this matter.

The following recommendations were approved by the church for this pastor only:

1. That Dr. Benjamin W. Robertson would remain General Chairman of the Trustees of this church for the duration of his pastorate. 297 affirmatives and 27 negatives (Passed by more that 90%).

2. That Dr. Benjamin W. Robertson will be in charge of the Administrative and the Spiritual parts of this church, and the Deacons and Trustees will assist him. 297 Affirmatives and 23 negatives (Passed by more than 90%).

3. That Dr. Benjamin W. Robertson will be given the authority to replace any disgruntled officer who is hindering the progress of the church and excommunicate them if necessary. 296 Affirmatives and 15 negatives (Passed by more than 90%).

All of this Pastoral Authority will come to an end when the Administration of Dr. Benjamin W. Robertson comes to an end. The new pastor will have to earn this kind of confidence.

Benediction by Dr. Floyd Davis

TRUST AND CONFIDENCE

(I have not abused any of this authority but have used it faithfully.) I have found out that if a pastor does his job, he will have the trust of the congregation. Most of these persons who had followed this educator and lawyer recognized that even though this pastor is not perfect, he is far better in the driver's seat than these persons who wanted to take over. I have included this in the book to let the young preacher know that if God is with you, nobody can hurt you. For He promised to be with me and He is. We thank God that we recognized this danger and were able to correct it before it got out of hand. Churches have been very careful of giving all the attention to the persons whom they have put on the Deacon Board and not as much attention as to the persons who are selected for trustees of the church. Many trustees are selected because of their training and financial strength with very little attention to their dedication to God and His church. Therefore, the church ends up with persons who are worldly in their decisions and pastor-competitors for the leadership of the church.

I must say that the trustees that we have on the board today are men and women whom I believe are born again by the Spirit of God, persons who respect the position of the pastor and make all decisions with God, His church and His under-shepherd in mind.

We found that the best way to select trustees is to have the pastor, the members of the Administrative Board (composed of all the deacons and trustees), to approve of all candidates before they are presented to the church. If the pastor recommends a person and the Administrative Board does not, that person will never come before the church. If the Administrative Board has a candidate for Board of Trustees and the pastor does not approve of that person, that person will never come before the church. Any person who comes on the board with the pastor or the others members not recommending him or her is trouble to start with. Many ministers have resigned pastorates and gone out to organize churches because their leadership has been rejected by officers with carnal minds who attempt to carry on spiritual work by secular means.

Since this conference, we have had very smooth sailing. I appointed Deacon Lloyd A. Jones chairman of the Building Committee for the erection of our Fellowship Hall. Deacon Jones and his committee have done an excellent job. The educator of whom we spoke had a change of attitude and has meant a lot to my ministry. Cedar Street is fortunate to have so many members who have so many talents. They have done many nice things which have helped me remain as long as I have.

THE SHOCK OF OUR LIVES

Sugar and I received the shock of our lives when at the age of sixty-six years, I received a registered letter from the Comonwealth of Virginia, Department of Social Services, Division of Child Support Enforcement. I had been named as the putative father of a child that I did not know. At first, I thought it was a joke. But when I called the office of the Division of Child Support, I found out that it was not a joke.

Sugar and I went to the Richmond District Office on East Franklin Street and talked with the man in charge. He was very nice in informing us of why they had to take the action that they did. He said that whenever an accusation is made that a man is the putative father, they must proceed to find out if it is true or not. And if it is true, legal terms will start to make the father support his child. If he is not the putative father of the child, everything will be dismissed. He informed us that the summons had been sent to me by the request of the child's grandmother who actually believed her daughter who told her that the pastor of Cedar Street was the father of her child.

A date was set for me to have the blood test. Sugar did not go with me when I went to have my blood tested. They gave me the works as if I were a prisoner. They took my picture, fingerprints, and social security number. As I was sitting there, one of our Sunday School teachers came in and talked with me. She expressed her confidence and the faith she had in me. I was embarrassed, but I knew that I had to prove that I was not the putative father of this child. For the Lord had blessed me to be the father of only one son, Benjamin W. Robertson Jr.

This had been on their record for some time but no one had tried to do anything about it. I remember that one of our members told me that a social worker told her that she "knew" that I was the father of a child but she would lose her job if it were found out that she revealed it. The member told this social worker that she did not believe her because, "What mother would support a child on welfare and permit a man who owns as much as Sugar and me get away from supporting a child of mine?" We were informed that the child was eleven years old.

Second, when it came to me who this grandmother was who took out the summons on me, I remembered her and her daughter. They were on welfare and would call from time to time to get help from our Missionary Ministry. She would send this daughter, who was accusing me of being the father of her child, to get the check from the church charity funds. This girl had dropped out of school and appeared to be a slow learner. It seems that when this child got pregnant, to keep the blame off herself, she named a community leader as the father of her child. This further made her feel good that a man of such standing would even want her.

However, when it came to attempting to prove it, she knew it wasn't true; therefore, she never wanted to seek child support. The mother of this child didn't want the grandmother to take any action because she knew what the outcome would be. The grandmother was taking her daughter's word. The mother of this child did not take the blood test because she knew that I had never had any sexual relations with her.

A Division of the Genetics and IVF Institute evaluated the test. This is what I received in mail:

> Benjamin W. Robertson
> 8901 Strath Road
> Richmond, Virginia 23231
>
> On 04/30/97 you agreed to submit to scientifically reliable genetic tests, including blood tests, for the purpose of proving that you are, or are not, the biological father of ———.
>
> On 06/06/1997 the results of your genetic test were returned to this office.
>
> The genetic blood test results indicated that there is zero (0) percentage probability of your being the father. Therefore, the summary of findings state that Benjamin Robertson is NOT the biological father of ———.
>
> This case is closed by the Division of Child Support Enforcement.

What they actually thought is that to keep it from becoming public I would have given support to this needy family. I am glad that this came to a head. The Commonwealth of Virginia Department of Social Services, Division of Child Support Enforcement has a record to show that I was not the biological father of this child.

I have included this case in the book to let the young preachers know that there are times when one must not try to hide anything. It was suggested to me that in order to keep down any bad publicity, I could voluntarily give the child four or five hundred dollars a month and never miss it. But I knew that if you are right, you don't have to give in to Satan's suggestions.

While I was fighting this charge on the one side, I was being honored on the other side. I had recently been appointed by the Honorable Governor George E. Allen to the State Board of Psychology; TV Channel 35 had honored me for Outstanding Contributions to Humanity; TV Channel 12 honored me as being a role model for the youth; Virginia Union University was about to confer on me the Honorary Degree of Doctor of Humane Letters; Sugar and I were about to celebrate forty-two years as pastor and first lady of one of the largest local congregation in the United States, and the Defense General Supply had made me an honorary chaplain.

After almost fifty years in the ministry, I can truly say that God has been true to His promise. He has given me so many friends who have helped in this pastorate. As I gather closer to the Jordan and sometimes can almost hear the sound from the waves and as my physical strength wanes, I have felt a renewed commitment to my God and to His causes. We have had many assistants to the pastor who have helped me greatly. These were men and women who did not look for glory but wanted to help in whatever way they could. Some of the assistants to the pastor and pulpit assistants were the Reverends S. M. Garnett, Harry F. Washington, Willie C. Thompson, Louis R. Blakey, Robert Woolridge, Floyd D. Davis, Ronald C. Taylor, Phillip Williams, Gerald A. Grandison, Alfred Jones, Joseph C. Seay III, Curtis Holt, Leroy Booker, Clarence Diggs, Andrew C. Epps Sr., Robert Lewis, Irvin Vice Jr., Arthur Roots, Ricky Brown, Fred Hannah, Robert Farmer, Louise Mills, Clara Morton, James White, Robert White, James E. Turner, Blanche Brown, Stanley Faison, Melvin Parham, Mabel Clark, Barbara Burroughs, Alvin A. Edwards, James Richardson, Shirlie McQuinn, Barbara Taylor, Delores Robinson, Jerome Pratt, Frank McLaurin Jr., James Ward Jr., Rico Patterson, Peyton Butler, Joseph Lee, K. L. Brazil, J. W. Green, David Haden, Isadore Mims, Sanford Williams, Emmanuel C. Harris, Deborah Burton, Jesse Butler, Johnnie H, Underwood Sr., A. Carl Prince, Ernest Blue, Thurman Williams, James Johnson, Charles Jackson III, Charles Calloway Jr., and Joseph Godfrey.

Cedar Street has been blessed because the Baptist Ministers have permitted the Metro-Revival to bring some of the greatest preachers in the country to the pulpit of Cedar Street. Such giants as Dr. E. V. Hill of California and Dr. Henry Lyons, president of the National Baptist Convention, U.S.A., Incorporated, served as the evangelists. Such preachers as Dr. Gardner C. Taylor, Dr. T. M. Chambers, Dr. J. Raymond Henderson, Dr. Vernon Johns, Dr. E. C. Smith, Dr. H. Beecher Hick Jr., Dr. Gordon B. Hancock, Dr. Charles Adams, Dr. M. C. Allen, Dr. Harold Carter, Dr. Noel C. Taylor, Dr. Charles Hart, Dr. Percy High, Dr. Leamon White, and many, many others have been heard from the pulpit of Cedar Street Baptist Church of God. It has been our desire to bring the very best we could find to serve this congregation.

CHAPTER SEVEN

The Future

AT THE TIME OF THE THIS WRITING, I AM AWARE THAT there will come a time for me to retire from the pastorate of Cedar Street Baptist Church of God. The church has provided for me to retire when the Lord has shown us that the time has come. I am observing four things. I feel that I should retire before the time comes that when I am preaching and it seems that the people are not getting the message, or when I look around each Sunday and see that there are more and more vacant pews, or when the offerings drop off so that it becomes hard to meet the obligations of the church, or when physically I am not able to carry on a reasonable part of the work of the pastorate. At the time of this writing all four indicators seem to be working pretty well. It seems as if the people are still understanding the message, the church is comfortably filled each Sunday, the offerings are of such that we can continue to grow, and I have a reasonable portion of health and strength. I am already extremely blessed to have served this long in the same pastorate with such fine people. However the plan is that we will begin to hear preachers after June 1, 1998.

Three of my friends who have retired in Richmond are doing more preaching and are in demand just as much as they were when they were in the pastorate. They are Dr. Robert L. Taylor, pastor

Dr. Benjamin W. Robertson Sr.

emeritus of the Fourth Baptist Church; Dr. E. D. McCreary Jr., pastor emeritus of Mount Carmel Baptist Church; and Dr. G. G. Campbell, pastor emeritus of Moore Street Baptist Church. Of course, these men are unusual pastors and preachers. All of them have served in the pastorate and at the same time served as teachers in seminaries in our city. It is a blessing for churches looking for a minister to supply the pulpit during the time the church is in search for a pastor with qualified men of experience and wisdom as these men are. Many of the churches that they have supplied wished it were possible for them to get these ministers to become their pastor. Most of them supplied service longer than they anticipated because the people were enjoying such rich experience and wisdom.

I mentioned near the front of this book the great preachers who served the pulpits in Richmond in 1955 when I came to the pastorate of Cedar Street. I want you to know that Richmond is presently served by great preachers and pastors and that I am confident that God will continue to call men and women to carry on His great work. Two churches in Richmond are served in the pastorate by women, Dr. P. Gould-Champ and the Reverend Linda B. Stevens, who are doing very well in those churches.

The great thing about the Kingdom of God is that God has always had somebody to step right in when the other has finished His work. The Richmond churches are doing fine and the preachers are still preaching the Gospel. After forty two years in the same pastorate, I know that most of my pastorate has been served.

I hope that the reader has been able to get something from the experiences that I have mentioned during our pastorate and have shared with you. What I have tried to show you is that God has been true to His promise when He gave the Great Commission in Matthew 28:18-20,

> And Jesus came and spake unto them, saying, All power is given unto me in heaven and in earth. Go ye, therefore, and teach all nations, baptizing them in the name of the Father and of the Son, and of the Holy Ghost: Teaching them to observe all things whatsoever I have commanded you: and, lo, I am with you always, even unto the end of the world.

That is the greatest promissory note that I have ever read.

I have just returned from Washington, D.C., where Sugar and I were with our friends, Dr. and Mrs. Leamon W. White. We always enjoy their company and the words of wisdom that he shares with us from his forty-four years of successful pastorate of the Mount Bethel Baptist Church. Dr. and Mrs. White have given much to help those who need it most.

You see, each person takes his position on the side of the mountain of life, and from his standpoint, God wants him/her to tell the world what he/she has seen. No one can tell what God has shown an individual, if he fails to tell it. I have just attempted to tell what God has shown me.

We are not concerned with how long now. We just want to be faithful until our work is finished. You may have recognized that *we* has been used instead of *I*. I have not been alone these forty-two years, but I have known that God has been with me and there has been a darling wife who has been more than a wife to me. She has kept her part all the way. I want it to be known that I have had so much help in this pastorate.

Everything that has been accomplished during our pastorate has been built on the shoulders of those who have gone on ahead of me. Some years ago, I heard the story of a young preacher who was sent on Sunday morning to a church in which he had to go around the side of the mountain to get there. He had to leave his horse and wagon at the foot of the mountain and travel by foot across the mountain. As he was walking in the little path that led to the other side of the mountain, he saw a snake in the pathway. He had to stay in the path because the mountain was too steep to go up or down.

He waited hoping that someone would come by to kill the snake that was in his path. He was a city man and did not know much about killing snakes. He knew that his time was limited because the hour of worship was nearing. He picked up a few rocks that were on the side of the mountain and began to walk slowly toward the snake. When he drew back to hit the snake's head, he discovered that the snake was already bruised. He knew then, that somebody had gone on ahead of him and made it possible for him to get to the church.

Every time there appears to be trouble in my pathway, I discover that somebody has gone on ahead me. After the Father, the Son, and the Holy Ghost, I have had the benefit of some fine pastors who have given me the privilege of building on their shoulders.

THE FORMER PASTORS OF CEDAR STREET

The Reverend Robert C. Kemp (1869–1877) 8 years
The Reverend Thomas Briggs (1878–1885) 7 years
The Reverend Jacob Turner (1886–1897) 11 years
The Reverend O. Paul Thompson (1898–1911) 13 years
The Reverend William Gray Sr. (1912–1915) 3 years
The Reverend William Harris Sr. (1915–1917) 2 years
The Reverend James H. Roots Sr. (1918–1940) 22 years
The Reverend John W. Kemp Sr. (1942–1954) 12 years

I am the ninth pastor and I have been here since 1955.

NOTABLE RICHMOND PASTORS

There have been only twelve pastors who have served the same Black Baptist congregation in the city of Richmond for forty or more years.

Dr. Anthony Binga, First Baptist Church, South Richmond
Dr. A. W. Brown, Sixth Mt. Zion Baptist Church
Dr. W. T. Johnson, First African Baptist Church
The Reverend Edward Jones, Mount Sinai Baptist Church
Dr. Cary S. McCall, Mount Tabor Baptist Church
Dr. Evans Payne, Fourth Baptist Church
Dr. W. L. Ransome, First Baptist Church, South Richmond
Dr. L. R. Taylor, Mount Vernon Baptist Church
Dr. S. M. Thompson, Mount Moriah Baptist Church
The Reverend H. W. Washington, Sharon Baptist Church
Dr. J. J. Woodson, Providence Baptist Church

In 1995, I made the twelfth pastor to have served for forty years in a Black Baptist Church in Richmond, Virginia. It makes me feel a little strange to be in a group where all have gone to the great beyond except me.

Dr. C. S. McCall served longer in the same pastorate of any Black Baptist Church in the history of the city of Richmond. He served for fifty years at the Mount Tabor Baptist Church.

OUR GOD CHILDREN

Sugar and I are happy to have six wonderful children to be our godchildren. Our first godchild is Tracy Grasty, the daughter of Mr. and Mrs. William Grasty; the second is Ronald C. Taylor Jr., the son of the Reverend and Mrs. Ronald C. Taylor Sr.; the third is Chaundra Carlette Davis, the daughter of the Reverend and Mrs. F. D. Davis, the fourth is Gerleta Dionne Grandison, daughter of the Reverend and Mrs. Gerald Grandison; the fifth is Vonzelle Waller, the daughter of Mr. and Mrs. Wythe Waller; and the sixth is Kenneth W. Crandell Jr., the son of Mr. and Mrs. Kenneth W. Crandell Sr.

CHAPTER EIGHT

When Faith Breaks Down

But when he noticed the strong wind, he became frightened, and beginning to sink, he cried out, Lord, save me.—Matthew 14:30

SOMEONE HAS SAID THAT IT IS HARD TO IMPROVE ON THE definition of faith that is given by the writer to the Hebrews. He says, "Faith is the substance of things hoped for, the evidence of things not seen."

Napoleon said, "All the scholastic scaffolding falls, as a ruined edifice, before one single word, and that word is faith." Another has said, "Faith marches at the head of the army of progress. It is found beside the most refined life, the freest government, the profoundest philosophy, the noblest poetry and the purest humanity." Another sees faith in an all-seeing God as a force that "elevates the soul, purifies the emotions and sustains human dignity."

So you can easily see that when faith fails, we do not have but very little left, and the going is destined to become more difficult as the days come and go. Without faith, we do not live; we simply exist. Without faith, hope is bound to die and courage will languish like a sickly vegetable in a desert place. But with faith, we enjoy abundant living. With faith, hope waxes strong and courage flourishes like a green bay tree.

One can easily distinguish the persons who live in the category of implicit faith and trust from the person who exists on the ragged edge of doubt. Faith gives one a happy countenance, whereas dead faith leaves a sad countenance. God has fixed man so that his mental attitude registers in his facial expressions. One can see faith working by the efforts one shows in the cause. When a person's faith breaks down, it will certainly change his attitude. When faith breaks down, it is the result of one's inability to stand the impact of life.

It is easy to have faith in God, in your fellow man, and in yourself when all goes well. But nothing but the pure in heart can remain faithful when disappointments rise on every side and the winds of opposition blow hard. It is not so easy to keep full of faith when you do the best you can and those around you misunderstand what you are trying to do.

The text presents Peter's faith unable to stand the impact of the occasion. The twelve had tried a sea voyage while Jesus was on the mountain alone at prayer. Jesus saw the ship as it was tossed and driven by some contrary winds. He knew that fear was in the hearts of the twelve.

Matthew writes that this was immediately after Jesus had fed the great multitude of people. They had immediately gotten into the boat and started to the other side while Jesus was dismissing the crowd. After Jesus had dismissed the crowd, He went up into the mountain by himself to pray. When evening came, Jesus was alone. But the disciples were in a little boat, and the boat was battered by the waves. They were far from the land, and they had encountered a strong wind.

Early the next morning, Jesus went to be with the disciples. When the disciples saw Him, He was walking on the sea. They were terrified and said to each other, "It is a ghost." And the Bible records that they cried out in fear. But immediately, Jesus spoke to them and said, "Take heart, it is I, do not be afraid." Peter answered "Jesus, Lord, if it is you, command me to come to you on the water." And Jesus said, "Come." So Peter got out of the boat. He had enough faith to get out of the boat while the boat was in the sea. He had so much faith that he started to go to Jesus who was out in the sea.

While Peter's mind was on Jesus, Peter was actually walking the water. The Bible says that he got out of the boat and started walking on the water and was coming toward Jesus. He had gotten out of the boat, that is important. He started to walking on the water, that is important. He was going to meet Jesus, that is very important. Just examine our lives. When we look to Jesus, we can do many miracles in His name. When we look to Jesus, our worries are lessened.

What happened to Peter happens to so many people. Peter believed that was the Lord and he knew of His power. For Peter had just seen Him feed five thousand men beside the women and children. Jesus had been preaching all day. When the disciples thought that the worship service was lasting too long, some were thinking that Jesus was a good preacher but a poor administrator. They somehow wanted to take over and do what they thought was best for the people. They informed Jesus that the night was coming, the town was too far and they didn't have enough money to buy food for such a great multitude of people. They further informed this poor administrator that all they had was a lad's lunch with two little fishes and five barley loaves. But Jesus said, "The people need not go away, you give them something to eat." They were so surprised and they replied to Jesus, "We have nothing here but five loaves and two fish." With the lad's lunch, Jesus fed that great multitude.

So you can see that Peter had a right to walk on the water to Jesus because he knew then that Jesus is the Messiah. Yet the Bible says that Peter in the midst of his walking, in the midst of his doing what is right, noticed the strong wind and became frightened and began to sink.

But thank God, Peter knew the one on whom he could depend, so he cried out, "Lord, save me." And immediately, Jesus stretched forth His hand and caught Peter. And said unto him, "O man of little faith! What made you lose your nerve like that?" Peter had learned that his own strength was not enough, and that he had to depend on Jesus. This is a lesson that all Christians are permitted to learn by experience.

We learn that Jesus comes to His people in the storms of life to deliver them. The Christians' duties are often difficult and self-denying. Nevertheless, he must do the will of God and leave events and results to an all-wise God. Sometimes in the midst of discharging of our duties, we are overtaken by a storm which not only obstructs our progress, but endangers our lives.

In elucidating the miraculous interposition of Jesus on their behalf, we see that Jesus exercised power when He came walking on the sea. There is no state in which Christ cannot save us. Our difficulties may be greatly multiplied and appear utterly insurmountable; but His hands are always long enough to save us. His ear is never too heavy that it cannot hear. It does not matter how distressing our fears may be for a moment—we shall have reason to be thankful for them. For most of the time, if we just observe, we recognize that as the means of impressing us with a more abiding sense of Christ's love and faithfulness. The God who "made the depths of the sea a way for the ransomed to pass over" and "saved Jonah in the belly of a fish" can never be at a loss for means to deliver us. On the contrary, the greater the obstacles to our salvation, the more God magnifies His power and grace in effecting it.

When Peter's faith broke down, he decided to pray, "Lord, save me." My brethren and sisters, let us never forget the power of prayer. Prayer is always in order. You don't have to be afraid of a praying man. You remember Saul who was threatening the followers of Christ. He went to the high priest and received letters to go to Damascus to persecute those in the synagogues. These letters would give him the permission to get men and women who were a part of this movement and bring them bound unto Jerusalem. But on his journey, he was stopped by the sudden flash of light that came from the sky. This light was brighter than the noonday sun. He also heard a voice. As he fell to the ground, this voice was saying, "Saul, Saul, why do you persecute me?" "Tell me, Lord," Saul said, "who are you?" The voice answered, "I am Jesus whom you are persecuting." "But get up and go into the city, and you will be told what you have to do." Meanwhile the men who were traveling with Saul stood speechless, they heard the voice but could see no one. Saul got up from the ground, but when he opened his eyes, he could not see. So they led Saul by the hand

and brought him into Damascus. He was blind for three days and ate no food nor did he drink anything.

The Lord had already spoken to one of His disciples, Ananias, who lived in Damascus. Ananias said, "Here I am, Lord." And the Lord said to him, "Rise and go to the street called Straight, and inquire in the house of Judas for a man of Tarsus named Saul. I want you to go and lay hands on him that he might regain his sight." Ananias answered, "Lord, I have heard about this man and all the harm he has done to the people in Jerusalem. And he is here with authority from the chief priest to arrest all who invoke thy name." But the Lord said to him, "You must go, for this man is my chosen instrument to bring my name before the nations and their kings, and before the people of Israel. Ananias, this man prays." After Ananias heard that this man had prayed, he went and laid hands on Saul and said, "Saul, my brother, the Lord Jesus, who appeared to you on your way here, has sent me to you so that you may recover your sight, and be filled with the Holy Spirit." And immediately it seemed that scales fell from his eyes, and he regained his sight. He was baptized, and afterward he took food and received his strength.

At some point in life, we all will face difficulties. Sometimes we are almost drowned by difficulties because we have over emphasized them. Let's look back and take another look. Notice a key expression in this passage: "But when he saw the wind was boisterous, he was afraid." It was not until Peter noticed the wind and began to over emphasize its importance that he really got into trouble. When Peter became possessed with the problem of walking on the water, in the midst of the wind and the waves, he failed. As long as he kept his eyes on Jesus and did not concentrate on the problem of staying up, he was safe. But when he let the problem become the primary thing, he sank.

After making a show of courage which transcended the test of the disciples, Peter must have been humiliated when he failed. Jesus rebuked him by saying, "Peter. What little faith! What made you lose your nerve like that?" Jesus did not embarrass him; He merely reached out His hand and caught him. Then they climbed into the boat and the wind ceased and all was calm. Once Jesus was settled in the boat, the disciples had a fresh glimpse of His greatness. They worshiped Him, saying, "Truly, you are the Son of God."

If the darkness of the night and the fury of the storms are upon us and we are beginning to sink into despair and doubt, we can cry to the Lord, "Lord, save me. I am sinking, save me." For the eyes of the Lord are upon us and when we have reached our extremity, He is right there to take over and to help us to carry our load.

There is a story that is told of a boy who went to the old fashioned Revival Service for the first time. This was back in the days when we had mourners' benches in churches. When revival time came, the front bench where the deacons usually sat was reserved for persons who were sinners or back-sliders to come near the pulpit. The reason for bringing them to the front was that they could hear the sermon without any interruption or distractions.

One night this boy came and sat on the mourners' bench at the request of the evangelist. He listened to the preaching and the singing, and he observed every question that was asked him by those church leaders. The boy remembers very well a question that one of the elderly ladies had asked him. As others were getting up from the mourners' bench, this boy just sat there. He remembered that as he sat there, a lady asked him a question that disturbed him greatly: "Boy, do you know God?" He went home and went to bed, but he could not sleep. For all during the night that question stayed on his mind, "Boy, do you know God?" The next morning when he got up, he did not want any breakfast. He came into the room where his mother was and with a loud voice asked, "Mama, do you know God?"

That same question kept ringing in his mother's ears all day long, "Mama, do you know God?" The mother was not able to do any housework that morning. About noon, she got in the car and started to riding around trying to erase that question from her mind. For even the motor from the car seemed to have asked her that same question. She came back home and just sat there.

When her husband came home, he wanted to know what was wrong with his wife. No breakfast dishes had been washed, no floors had been swept, no supper had been cooked, and she did not meet him at the door with the usual smile. When he inquired, she told him the question that had been bothering her all day. The husband said, "Why didn't you tell the boy how long you have been a member of the church?" She said, "Husband, he didn't ask me that." "Why didn't you tell him how you worked in the Red Cross and all the community work that you have done, the Sunday School class you are teaching each Sunday morning?" She said, "He didn't ask me that, he wanted to know if I knew God."

My friends, there is a whole lot of difference in how long one has been a member of a church, what work he has done in the community, and whether one knows God or not. Somewhere in one's life, he should have had an encounter with God.

CHAPTER NINE

The Called and the Sent

IT WAS NOT MY DESIRE TO BE THE FOUNDER OF THE Richmond Virginia Seminary. It appeared that it was God who wanted me to do more than the work of the local pastorate. We had just completed the building of the main sanctuary of the Cedar Street Baptist Church of God when the Search Committee of Virginia Seminary & College in Lynchburg met in Baltimore, Maryland, and invited me to come to the meeting. Sugar and I drove to Baltimore to find out why they wanted me to meet with them.

My first thought was that the Search Committee had a recommendation and wanted to get my opinion since Cedar Street was one of the larger supporters of the seminary. But to my surprise, they wanted me to be the acting president of Virginia Seminary & College. During the discussion, someone suggested that I would become the tenth president in order that I might have some authority to operate the institution properly. Here I was being asked to do something that I knew very little about. When I got to the car and told Sugar what they wanted. She said, "That was nice of them, but I know that you did not accept it." When I told her that I accepted, she said, "Daddy, are you crazy?" She continued by saying, "How can you be the pastor of a church in Richmond and president of a school in Lynchburg?"

The real problem was that the school had no students, and I was called in to begin a work of which I had no experience. But when we left there after a few months, there was a student body of twenty-three and more than $40,000 in the bank. While I was in the president's office, I found some books on small colleges, private schools, and religious institutions which I enjoyed reading. Sugar was right, it was too far away from the church to do anything worthwhile. So I resigned and came back to Richmond.

Somehow, the presidential challenge was in my blood. So I used what I had learned in those few months to start the Richmond Virginia Seminary. There were several things that I employed to test the waters before I opened the doors. I wanted to have a school that could confer degrees, so I started with the Council of Higher Education of the State of Virginia. After we were approved to confer the bachelor, master and doctorate degrees in Religion, we were approved by the Veteran's Administration and the Internal Revenue Service as a non-profit organization.

Many of the Richmond pastors became supporters of the work at the start along with Dr. Charles Hart and Dr. Frank Guns in Norfolk, Dr. E. C. Smith and Dr. Leaman White in Washington, D.C., Dr. W. Franklin Richardson and Dr. Ollie Wells in New York, Dr. Stacy Williams in Michigan, Dr. Harold Carter and Dr. A. C. D. Vaughan in Maryland, and Dr. Percy High in North Carolina. I was very much encouraged when I received a letter from Dr. David T. Shannon, president of Virginia Union University, stating that he thought there is a need for a seminary that would take persons where they are and lead them higher.

Of course, the seminary met with some opposition. One minister said to me that since Virginia Union University is doing such a good job there is no need to have another school doing the same work. He expressed the idea that if one is doing very well why start another. He felt that all the little seminaries ought to close up and encourage their students to go to the established school. I asked him if he thought that all the little churches ought to close and send the few members that they had to the big churches. You know what his answer was. Then he jumped on accreditation. I told him that the School of Religion at Virginia Union University had produced some of the best preachers in the country before it was fully accredited in 1970. At that time neither the School of Religion at Shaw nor Virginia Seminary and College were accredited, and Bishop College had just lost its accreditation. Yet those four religious schools have given the churches of this country some of the finest pastors in the world. I don't know when the Richmond Virginia Seminary will become a fully accredited seminary, but that is our goal. We are candidates for accreditation with the Transnational Association of Christian Colleges and Schools (TRACS).

I have discovered that the bigger the heart of a person, the more consideration that he gives in helping other institutions to become greater. Richmond Virginia Seminary has always had good faculty members. Most of the instructors are graduates of Virginia Union University. To name a few: Dr. Robert L. Taylor, Dr. Robert Williams, Dr. Joseph Godfrey, Dr. Dennis Thomas, Dr. Dolores Llewellyn, Dr. Yvonne Bibbs, Dr. Matthew Johnson, Dr. B. Clark-Jones, Dr. Lutrelle Rainey, Dr. Robert Pettis, Dr. V. W. Hylton, Dr. Willie Carter, Dr. James Lynch, Dr. Roy West, and Attorney Rosemary Harris. We have had three academic deans, Dr. George L. Jones, Dr. Peyton Butler, and presently serving, Dr. Clifton Whitaker Jr. Mrs. Joyce R. Baker is the director of records. Other staff persons are Mrs. Josephine Gordon, Michael White, and Mrs. Debbie Taylor. Dr. Herbert Plummer and Dr. E. L. Fleming serve as chairmen of our Board of Trustees. Dr. A. Lincoln James is our vice-president.

DONALD L. SMITH DORMITORY

We are now preparing to break ground for our new Donald L. Smith Dormitory. Dr. Smith is a graduate of our seminary and has built one of the outstanding religious institutions in Virginia. This new dormitory will have two stories to serve both our male and female students. We are nearing the maximum enrollment that the city will allow for occupancy of the building. This dorm will cost more than $600,000 when completed.

SHARING THE RESPONSIBILITIES

If a pastor is able to get the members of the church to know that they are needed and each has a job to do, much can be accomplished for the Lord. The illustration is given of a large firm that placed a sign in the window stating that help is wanted. A hundred persons applied at the office to seek employment in that firm. They were all employed and told to report to work in about a week. When they arrived the next week, each was wearing his work clothes and ready to go to work. It was the foreman's job to tell each person just where to work and what to do. They were called about a week ago, but they still had to be assigned to their individual task. There are many types of workmen needed to erect a building. Each had to be assigned a specific job to do. There were many positions because of the wide range of work that was required to complete the whole job. The work must be harmonized and integrated so that there is no overlapping and no great parts of the job left alone.

Likewise the church needs a wide variety of ministries in order to accomplish the task of evangelizing the world.The church needs some frontline missionaries and evangelists who are devoted to a life of prayer. The church needs tithers who will give that tenth to help supply these frontline missionaries. The church needs some on the homefront as well as those who will go abroad. Most churches suffer for a need for Sunday School teachers and members in all departments. We have assigned to us by the Lord of harvest some work that no one can do if we fail. Thank God that we have the privilege and duty to perform whatever task that He assigns to us.

In Romans 12:4–18, we read,

> For as we have many members in one body; and all members have not the same office: so we, being many, are one body in

Christ, and every one members one of another. Having then gifts differing according to the grace that is given to us, whether prophecy, let us prophesy according to the proportion of faith; or ministry, let us wait on our ministering; or he that teaches, on teaching; or that exhorts, on exhortation; he that gives, let him give it with simplicity; he that rules, with diligence; he that shows mercy, with cheerfulness.

THE CALLED AND SENT

The early disciples had been called away from secular employment to win souls for the Kingdom of God. Young David was anointed with oil that he should later become king over Israel. The Apostle Paul was called and chosen to bear Christ's name before the Gentiles and kings and the children of Israel. Each person who considers giving their lives to full-time Christian service should make sure that he has specific instructions from the Lord of harvest to make this choice. A false call or a running without being sent is indeed a most serious thing.

For one should never choose the ministry as a profession in order to gain social prestige or to have opportunity for the display of forensic abilities or to show social and moral leadership. One must be aware that a call to preach is a spiritual conception because the natural man cannot understand the things of the Spirit of God.

In Mark 3:13–15, we find both the "called and sent" according to the New King James Version, "And He went up on the mountain and *called* to Him those He Himself wanted. And they came to Him. Then He appointed twelve, that they might be with Him and that he might *send* them out to preach, and to have power to heal sicknesses and to cast out demons." For the call of God is a special call to special responsibilities. To be called of God is an honor above all honors with unlimited opportunities. Those who have been called must accept without regards to personal ambitions or financial aspirations or social prestige. The call of God affects the whole person, his actions, and his words.

This call is inaudible to the natural ear but is distinct and very clear to the heart of one who is born again. Isaiah said, "Thine ears shall hear a word behind thee, saying, this is the way, walk ye in it." There will be a definite whispering in the deepest soul that the child of God will be conscious of, and it will be his clarion call into the Lord's service. Elijah heard it, and it was called the "still small voice."

When one is called by God, God has always taken the initiative. Listen to Him, "Ye have not chosen Me, but I have chosen you, and ordained you, that ye should go and bring forth fruit, and that your fruit should remain: that whatsoever ye shall ask of the Father in My Name, He may give it to you" (John 15:16). To understand this clearly, we are in a better position to accept that call. God sees what we can do before He calls us. He knows our possibilities and our handicaps and calls us nevertheless into His Christian service. The old song is right, "He Knows Just How Much We Can Bear." We can be assured that God has figured it out and knows He can use us as one of His under-shepherds.

Some years ago, one of the deacons was attempting to doubt the calling of a preacher who had come by. In his remarks, he said, "God has more sense than I have. I would not send my son on a job without the proper tools to do the job. If I sent my son to paint a house, I would give him a some paint and some paint brushes. I would tell him the color for the house and a different color for the trim. I would teach him how to paint before I sent him on the job. I would give him my telephone number in case he had some problems and needed me." What he was saying made some sense. Before the call comes to a person, in most cases there will be a certain natural fitness for the work to which the Lord has called him. The call comes to an individual with a voice that is not difficult to understand and an appearance that is not objectionable, and an average amount of ability to think and to express oneself, which make good material for the Lord to use.

Therefore, churches seldom call persons to be their pastor who cannot preach. It has been said the preaching is the central, primary, decisive function of the church. When the congregation gathers on the Lord's day in worship, there will be many important things that are involved in the worship. However, what makes the worship service what it should be is the preaching of the Gospel. The fervent prayer prayed by the deacon, the reading from the Holy Bible, and the good singing help, but it's the preaching that builds strong, solid Christians.

Preaching is not a function apart from worship and is not a one-man function. It is not the preacher alone who worships God through the message. The whole congregation worships as the Gospel is being preached.

So I close by saying,"Preach on, Preacher," and may the Lord use you mightily in His service. In almost fifty years of preaching, I can truly say that the Lord has been "Just as He promised." Someone has said that the sermon is "the organized Hallelujah" of the church.

CHAPTER TEN

Finding Fault with God

THE FOLLOWING IS A SERMON PREACHED BY DR. JUNIUS C. Austin Sr. in 1939 at the Board Meeting of the National Baptist Convention, U.S.A., Incorporated in Hot Springs, Arkansas. Dr. J. C. Austin, pastor, Pilgrim Baptist Church, Chicago, was one of the country's great orators.

> Then he which had received the one talent came and said, "Lord, I knew thee that thou art an hard man, reaping where thou hast not sown, and gathering where thou hast not strawed. And I was afraid, and went and hid thy talent in the earth; lo, there thou hast that is thine." His lord answered and said unto him, "Thou wicked and slothful servant, thou knewest that I reap where I sowed not, and gather where I have not strawed. Thou oughtest therefore to have put my money to the exchangers, and then at my coming I should have received mine own with usury." (Matt. 25:24–27)

As students of life and the Word of God, we understand this is a parable out of which our lesson comes. A parable, or floodlight, thrown upon the great theme, "The Kingdom of heaven." A parable setting forth a code of ethics by which God would have us live. We have in this message the key, or secret, to the combination

Dr. Junius C. Austin Sr.

of successful living. Living is man's one and only problem—Just how to adjust ourselves to the proper fitness in the social order, just how to make our best contributions to the body politic, just how to find our fitness in the woof and weave of life garment, just how to get the most out of this thing called life was the burden of the master in every message. Therefore, He often spoke in parables knowing as He did that He was dealing with feeble-minded children, dumb and dull of understanding.

Listen now to the sensible, practical, commonplace illustration which sets forth the plan of man's salvation including within itself the thought of God and the attitude of His fallen, broken, and marred image, "I was afraid and went and hid thy talent in the earth." A textual study, or analytical investigation, will reveal to us that man is a depository of a great trust. He has within him the potentialities, the ingredients, the essential elements of the Kingdom of heaven. Man is a mighty territory, a universe, a wonderful world in which God delights to set up His throne and rule and reign to His own glory and to the salvation of this human Kingdom.

There is clearly set forth herein man's free moral agency. He is his own boss. In this parable, the only motivation for thrift and economy was the profitable return in the exchange of talents, or investments, and the approbation of the Master when he would return, and the final promotion and reward for fidelity in the discharge of duty.

I have often wondered about the disinterest God seems to manifest in human problems. I shall never forget my personal worries over the sinking of the Titanic and the suffering of Collins in the Kentucky cave years ago. I just felt that God should have done what I felt willing to do, glorify Himself in saving the situation. In the kidnaping of the Lindbergh's baby, I was anxious to see the delivering hand of God; or somewhere in the trial of Hauptmann, I listened for the voice of the Eternal One, but all of it passed as a mere routine in human experiences, with nothing supernatural revealing itself. Like the critics looking up into the bloody face of the Son of God when He was in the hands of the mob, I asked my soul, "Where is God?" I have been known to grumble and complain because it rained on Sunday, or on the day of a church picnic, and it was beautiful and clear on the following morning. A study of God and man has taught me that God gives us this world with all its storms, its dangers and catastrophes. This world with its black horse of sorrow, its red horse of carnage and blood, its pale horse of death, its white horse of Gospel conquest, and it is up to us to face the wind, tempest and tide, and conquer the forces of nature, or of hell.

Yes, man is God's partner in the running of the universe. There are things we must do, and there are things we must let God do. Finding the boundary of our activities, or of our extremities, is but to discover God's opportunity to work for us. God will never stand for any man unloading his failures and shortcomings on Him. We must give an account as stewards in operating this world.

Our endowments are knowledge and capacity of truth, talents, sense of duty, and righteousness. Within every man is a conscience in which is the whispering voice of the Infinite. Which if obeyed, will always steer him into the harbor of safety.

Other things among our assets are time, talent and strength. These are for this human organism of intellect, sensibility, and will, the things which make up this human personality. Please understand that time does not belong to us. We cannot give ourselves time. It is a spark flashed from eternity, from beneath the ringing hammer of Providence upon the anvil of the Holy purpose. It comes to us to be used as a most vital and essential gift of God. Talent is not ours. Whether we can sing, preach, or pray, we should remember that it "Cometh down from Him who giveth liberally and upbraideth not." We must give an account of our moments spent. How and where, and also of our talents.

Be it further known to you, your strength, whether in body or mind, is a gift from God. God gives wisdom, and hidden somewhere back of the ligaments, back of the tissues, down in the heart, and in the recesses of the spirit, is the generator of power operated by the Almighty God. Oh! My God! What will our answer be when God shall question us as to our days and nights and use of our powers?

Man does not create his opportunities. They come to him riding upon the tidal wave of time directed by the Good Man who walked upon the sea of Galilee; and it is ours to open the door and welcome opportunity for he will not return. One of the ancient writers says, "time has a lock of hair in his forehead to be grasped by wisdom, but when he passes he is so constructed with baldness there is nothing upon which you can rest your hand." May God help us to profit by the mistakes all of us have made in letting opportunity rich and replete with the blessings of God go by unnoticed.

Let me call your attention to the text in a practical way. The parable sets forth before us two characters. The first is styled as good and faithful. The other as wicked and slothful. Being so closely allied to the slothful character, or so much endangered by his folly, we shall consider him as the principle actor. By way of comparison, we notice one man is approved of God and promoted from servitude to ownership in heaven on the grounds that he was good and faithful. Observe, if you please, not on good scholarship, though he might have been brilliant and illustrious. Not on the grounds of heroic deeds, though he was noble. But on the grounds of goodness that revealed itself in faithfulness in serve. You know, friends, this thing is very encouraging to me. For it puts the possibility of pleasing God and winning heaven within reach of the most humble. I am not asked to match arms with the pugilist, Joe Louis, or the rich Rockefeller, or the militant Hitler, or the diplomatic Roosevelt. I am asked to do all I can with the little I have, to the glory of God and the good of my fellow man.

> The poor widow with her mite
> can serve to God's delight
> while the King with scepter in hand
> must live for the good of man.

Note, if you please, this other man out of whose life the big lesson comes. Wicked and slothful, he had a philosophy of life which is often observed among us. First of all, he felt very sure of himself. He felt he was right. He felt everybody else who did not see life as he saw it were fools. He was also brave and brazen in attitude. He did not hide his deeds; he walked right up and reported with more affrontage and arrogance than those who had done something worthwhile. Listen to his argument to God his master; "Now, Master, I am a smart man. I am brilliant. I know you, you are hard, reaping where you have not sown, and gathering where you have not strawed." The Greek rendition of this text is not, "I am afraid." But rather, "I am careful, exact, and did not take my chance. Therefore, I dug a hole and buried the talent. Here it is." Study the man. He worked harder to keep from working than any of the servants. He got himself a hoe and dug a grave. Now, why do I say grave?

He was burying a talent which is equivalent to 250 English pounds. He was burying a gift of God. He was burying the bridge that spanned the chasm between hell and heaven. He was burying an opportunity which would immortalize him throughout eternity.

To do this, he had to sink a shaft deep as hell. Now, the only thing I can say about him is, he worked through life digging a hole. He buried his soul in a hole.

Note the lesson; he did not plow a furrow, nor dig a ditch. This would have taken him out of self into the field of service. He just dug in one place in life. The character of this man is reflected in the failure of millions who feel they can get by on fault finding and excuses. They feel that laziness, passing the buck, and dodging responsibilities, is a smart act. But as was with this man, so be it with us. We have got to give an account of wasted energy and time.

I must close this lesson leaving upon your hearts this concluding thought. "The purpose of man in the scheme of life is to serve." He who would be great in the Kingdom must be the servant of all. Everything God has made is for service. God wasted no energy, no thought, no time in planning and building this world.

His stars, His rising suns and changing moons, His falling shadows, rifting clouds, and dawning days, His waving forest, heaving seas and bellowing storms, must all serve a purpose. From the crawling ant in the dust to the roaring lion in the den, from the canary singing in the trees to the eagle screaming in the rocks, from the rippling brook dancing and singing out of the mouth of spring, to the restless ocean rocking from the shore to shore, they must all serve. From the tallest archangel in heaven to the poorest peasant on the roadside of life, have service to be rendered. Shortly, all creation must come before God and give an account. In what class are you? Will you be found good and faithful or wicked and slothful?